SON OF ELWOOD

On Becoming Fatherless

By

Tom Bickimer

Lots of High Praise & Some Faint Praise for "Elwood"……….
(All made up of course, and all in good fun)

The Kansas City Times calls this "an important, spiritually uplifting book of puzzling popularity" while naming it to their Best Seller List.

Garrison Keillor, book reviewer for Lake Wobegon's The Herald Star, notes Bickimer's Oak Street family would feel right at home in Lake Wobegon. He states in his glowing review of "Elwood," "I only wish I could write as well as Bickimer."

Rolling Stone Magazine says the iconic music references in "Elwood" would make a kick-ass soundtrack . Rolling Stone concludes, "Bickimer is our next literary star."

The Wall Street Journal doesn't.

Oprah can't wait to have Bickimer on her show saying, "His book is a must read. A wonderful, heart-warming story everyone should read at least twice to understand what it is he's trying to say. This book will take you on a spiritual journey that will change your life. I just love this book."

Glenn Beck not so much. In fact, Beck calls Bickimer a bleeding-heart liberal whose book is Exhibit "A" for what's wrong with America today.

Jon Stewart exclaims that after reading "Elwood," "Bickimer is smart and funny, yet doesn't take himself too seriously like some people I know. He can come on my show anytime to discuss anything, except Glenn Beck."

It has been reported that both Bickimer and Rush Limbaugh worked at Royals Stadium back in the day. After reading the intellectual, inspiring "Elwood," Limbaugh admits he would NOT, "tie one hand behind his back" if he were to debate Bickimer. In fact, he really wants no part of Bickimer, ever.

The Holy Spirit Breakfast Club Literary Review names "Elwood" book of the year. The HSBCLR calls "Elwood" a literary master-piece, and goes on to say, "Bickimer has staked his place with the literary giants of all time. We award him a year's worth of free Thursday breakfasts." Of course, there's a malicious rumor going around that "Elwood" was the only book the HSBCLR read this year.

Upon reading "Elwood," Bickimer's mom goes public and admits for the first time that he was always her favorite child.

Bruce Springsteen calls the writing in "Elwood," "powerful stuff," and proclaims, "there's an album in there somewhere."

Rick Reilly wonders where this guy Bickimer has been hiding, "His writing is magnificent. Writing with humor and emotional honesty he somehow manages to seamlessly weave the diverse sporting worlds of football, baseball, basketball, wrestling and golf into the fabric of his story. 'Elwood' is a gold medal performance."

Bickimer's parish priest, Fr. Bishop, hard-pressed to recommend a more important spiritual book to read (after the Bible of course) wonders if perhaps it wouldn't have been easier for Bickimer to have just gone to confession.

Along the same lines, the esteemed (and awfully cute) literary critic Mary Helen Hamilton calls "Elwood" a great read. Maybe not to her taste in books, but still a great read. And oh, a story that should have been told 30-odd years ago, if the author had been more open and communicative. But then, there would have been no reason to write this book.

Son Of Elwood, On Becoming Fatherless is a work of nonfiction. Names, characters, places and incidents are real except on those rare occasions when the author's memory failed him. Author acknowledges some events maybe slightly out of sequence, but remarkably resemble actual events, people and locations.

Published by One to One Marketing LLC

www.1to1marketing-inc.com

Cover design by Mary and Tom Bickimer dba
M & T Productions

Special thanks to Carole Bickimer for permission to use her painting "Look At The Moon" on the back cover of this book.

The Library of Congress has yet to figure out how to categorize Tom Bickimer or his book Son of Elwood.... something about defying description.

Printed in the United States of America, thank goodness, no out-sourcing here.

10 9 8 7 6 5 4 3 2 1

www.promiseoflearning.com

Son of Elwood

On Becoming Fatherless

For

Mary
Carole, Mary, Leslie, Paul, and Laura
Tommy, Michael, Megan, Kristen, John, and Matthew
Dad, in memoriam

and those of you made fatherless too young in life

and lastly, honestly, myself

Author's Note:

I readily admit my memory is not the best. While reading this story, my Oak Street family may be amazed by how much I do remember, or equally appalled by how much I've forgotten, as I relate events that occurred 36 years ago. More than likely, there will be some muttering about how this or that didn't happen then, or it happened earlier or later or whatever. The important thing to keep in mind here, is everything mentioned did occur, and while maybe not in the correct chronological order, is true to my story. Yes, this story is autobiographical, and therefore is not meant to represent how my siblings or mother saw things at the time. If you should run into one of them, please be kind, it's not their fault I wrote this.

There are no do-overs in life, but there is the promise of learning.

5-5-10

Other Author's Notes of Less Importance

My conservative friends will be relieved to know that there were no illegal aliens employed in the writing of this book.

My liberal friends will be disappointed to learn no Federal funding was used for the publication of this book, and that I secretly harbor aspirations of making money off this book. They may be somewhat relieved to hear most of the gazillions I hope to make would go to charity. In fact, the entire net proceeds from the sales of this book will benefit The Promise of Learning Foundation.

My Christian Right friends may be a little leery of the swear words found in the book, but should be relieved to hear the Author has "K-Love" on one of his radio's preset buttons.

Lastly, I want to reassure my children that this is not hereditary.

Contents

Prologue

"All human wisdom is contained in these two words:
wait and hope."

"The Count of Monte Cristo"
Alexandre Dumas

"I know they say you can't go home again
I just had to come back one last time…

I thought if I could touch this place or feel it
This brokenness inside me might start healing…

If I could walk around, I swear I'll leave
Won't take nothing but a memory
From the house that built me"

From the song "The House That Built Me"
By Miranda Lambert
Written by Tom Douglass, Allen Shamblin

Time Traveler

Brian, "Augy" to those near and dear to him, was the closest I came to having a best friend since my days in high school. Of course, there is any number of us who could say the same thing, and we all have our Augy stories to prove it. We've heard the stories told and retold many times over in one shape or another while we were in one shape or another. We often figure in each other's stories, maybe that's why the stories don't grow old. We do, but the stories don't. I think most guys fall under the storyteller category. There are a chosen few who give the rest of us the stories to tell. Brian was one of the chosen few. It was Augy who gave us our camaraderie. He made new friends with the greatest of ease, I did not. He just as easily included his new buds in our ever-expanding merry band of Augy followers. I was content to be known as one of Augy's good friends, to be a member of the band.

With Brian and me, our friendship started with a confidence that we were, after all, masters of our respective universes. When we first met, we were 30-somethings who had great families and successful jobs. Brian was a financial planner, and somewhere along the line I became a client of his. We had common interests, particularly golf, and held common beliefs that started with a strong faith in God. We were competitive by nature, but Brian was much more good-natured about it. You could say we were idealistic but not annoyingly so. You could even say we both knew we were blessed way beyond what we deserved, so we felt compelled by Catholic guilt to give back in different ways when we could. Brian and I, even as we became 40-somethings, man, we had the tiger by the tail. There wasn't anything we couldn't do or accomplish. We were invincible. Sure, we had our differences and I usually came out on the short end of the competition thing, but at the end of the day, he was a great guy to share the stuff of life with. He was the most faith-filled, good-natured man I knew. As my best friend, there is no question he made me a better man.

I think those of us who knew Brian have what I call "best friend memories," a favorite personal memory or two of Augy we like to keep to ourselves. I know I do. Take the time we got together for what I thought would be a typical lunch for us, just two busy friends catching up on life and business. Before I knew what hit me, Brian had talked me into starting a charity golf tournament. There were lots of reasons not to do this, most of them coming from me. Couldn't we wait until we were less busy, had more money, more time, etc., etc. There was also the small detail that neither one of us had ever done anything like this before.

For Brian, none of it mattered. There was no time better than the present time. Besides, what we lacked in experience we made up for with glorious naiveté and enthusiasm. It still brings a smile to my face when I recall the memory of Augy and I careening around the golf course in a commandeered golf cart, taking aim at unsuspecting golfers who generally demanded quiet as they played, and letting them have it with a well-placed verbal barb amplified by a bullhorn we had some-how got our hands on. All of golf's stately decorum was out the window at that point, but we sure had a helluva good time.

The success that inaugural tournament, and the years that followed, were due in large part to Augy's huge circle of friends, and big heart. We did a lot of good with the money we raised from those tournaments.

There is one other story I carry in my heart I would like to share with you. Towards the end, Brian and his wife Sue stopped by the house one evening to pay us a visit and see our new baby. My wife Mary and I were foster parents for several years and Social Services had recently placed with us a newborn, Native-American baby we affectionately called Baby Louis. What made this night my favorite Augy memory was the sight of Brian holding that baby. In that singular moment in time, I saw a tidal wave of emotions wash over his being, a kaleidoscope of wonder and awe, wistfulness and yearning, sadness and joy, regret and pain. Lastly, I saw his immense appreciation for this gift of life, this gift of promise and hope that was Louis, held so tenderly by Brian in his arms. It was hard for Brian to let Baby Louis go.

Mary and I became foster parents because we loved children, and wanted to give kids in difficult circumstances a loving home for as long as they needed one. We did not foster in hopes of adopting. We welcomed kids into our home and said good-bye to a number of them over the years. But Baby Louis was different. He had stolen my heart. Like Brian, I didn't want to let him go. We found out, however, tribal law trumps our state's social service laws. We learned Native-American babies could only be adopted by people of the same race, no exceptions. Heart-broken, we lost Louis to cultural preservation laws. A short time later, we experienced heart-break again when we lost Brian to cancer.

On the first Monday of that October, a gorgeous Indian summer day, our group gathered for the annual golf tournament. It was the same group of friends, the same place, same time, same esprit de corps we had shared for years, all held together by the man we had come to honor that day. Before the start of the tournament, we assembled on the practice range, drivers in one hand and a specially marked ball in the other. Each of us had printed the word "Augy" on our golf balls, and with the precision of a military honor guard, we teed-off in unison. It was our version of a 21-gun salute to our departed dear friend. Henceforth, our golf tournament would have the word "Memorial" in its name.

Later that evening, we attended Brian's wake. A number of us got up and paid tribute to him. I remained firmly rooted in my pew, chagrined at my reluctance to publicly convey my appreciation for Augy's friendship and the love I held for him. I sat there humbled by the realization my grief was not the exclusive grief I alone could feel as Augy's best friend. I now saw there was nothing intimate or special about my grief. I should have known better. I looked around me at the sad faces of those who had gathered, and listened to heart-felt words spoken with broken voices. I came to understand my grief was a grief shared by many others who also called my best friend their best friend. His wife and daughters deserved to hear what I did not have the courage to say out loud about a husband and father too young for this kind of testimony. Too damn young. Too close to home. What the hell was I waiting for?

I'm thinking it's finally time. Circumstances, like my friend's passing, have conspired over the years to remind me I just might have something worthwhile to say. But I held back. Partly for fear of appearing pretentious, and partly because I was unwilling to make the emotional investment required. On those rare occasions when I didn't hold back, my tentative attempts often left me disappointed by their inadequacy. We've all been confronted with those occasions when we knew not what to say. When it was painfully obvious the depth of any words of comfort we could offer were no match for the depth of sorrow displayed before us.

36 years of reluctance is proof positive I hadn't been ready to raise my hand. These are the thoughts that come bubbling to the surface as I sit here in the comfort of my study, feeling the warm November sun as it streams through the windows. I look out to see the last vestiges of a rainbow autumn clinging stubbornly to balding trees waving in the wind. There's anticipation with knowing it's time.

The house is quiet, save the rhythmic "tick-tock, tick-tock" of the mantel clock's relentless count of time. My wife and I live in a beautiful home, embarrassingly too big now that the kids have grown and moved on. Our home is in a quiet, manicured, suburban neighborhood where privacy is guarded with an enthusiasm that puts one on the defensive if a neighbor should happen to approach while you're out in the yard. My home is not more than 10 minutes away from the house I grew up in. Defined as a measurement of length, the distance is a trivial amount. When defined as a measurement of time, well, that distance is a decades-long journey that's brought me to this beautiful fall day with time on my hands. Time, that relentless accounting of life that has finally eroded away my reluctance and left me resolved to speak of ghosts past and present. So here I am, perhaps in the autumn of my own life, and I'm thinking it's finally time to take a trip back in history with you. Buckle up, and let's get to it before I change my mind.

Cue some background music for this introduction, say, the theme from Stanley Kubrick's movie, "2001: Space Odyssey." Can you hear it? Ok, as the music plays, we see Mother Earth from somewhere out in space. We begin our travel back in time by googling the time machine earth.com and pulling up satellite images of our planet. (Ha! Look at that sentence I just wrote. No way I write that same sentence back where we're going.) I core down layer upon layer of time and matter: 9-11, Y2K, Operation Desert Storm, the world wide web, baby boomers, the generations Me and X, the fall of the Berlin Wall, Apollo 11, disco and Watergate. We journey earth to nation,

nation to state, state to city, and city to street. Finally, we arrive at the doorstep of a pastel-green two-story house guarded by pin oak sentinels in the front yard. This is my childhood home, circa 1974. Fade the intro music and begin the voice-over:

This is home to the story I'm ready to tell you about. I pray to tell it well. At the risk of sounding maybe just a little pretentious, I do think I have the benefit of a wisdom born of hard-earned experience honed by hindsight and reflection. I've waited a long time, 36 years worth of save-the-date reminders received each May. I trust the wait will hold me in good stead as I look back at a time that irrevocably changed who I was and who I was going to be. There is no story to tell without that date; I would not be the person I am today without that date. This is a story about a young man's crashing conclusion of childhood, and his sink-or-swim commencement of adulthood. Each of them bound to the other by a single, tragic event. I just want to do it justice, to have no regrets. I want to be true.

Let's see, "tragic event," i.e., tragedy. Let me make sure about this: Good ol' Mr. Webster defines tragedy as "a dramatic, disastrous event". Yup, that works. In and of itself, that event, which forms the foundation of my story, is neither unique nor exceptional in our world. Yet, give it context and a personal perspective, then maybe, by its very authenticity, the sum of my story will give hope to someone who can identify with it, and see how tremendously blessed I am to be the storyteller.

Once upon a time...

Chapter 1

"If I knew I were to die tomorrow,
I would plant a tree today."

Martin Luther

Dreams

When Ace reached his early teens, his nights were sometimes haunted by one particular dream theme: the sudden loss of his father. The storyline was pretty much the same thing: son dreams dad goes on a business trip, dad dies by some catastrophic event like a car or plane crash, son wakes with a start to find that, yes, everything seems to be alright, to still be in comforting order in the here and now. Ace's dad traveled a lot when he was growing up. He missed his dad, but I suppose those dreams could also be a manifestation of a son's fear that one day dad would not come home.

"Ace" was the nickname my father called me more often than my given Christian name. I was the oldest of his five children. We children were the product of, and witness to, a great love shared by my mother and father. Mom and dad had met and started their lives together in Fort Wayne, Indiana. Mom, born and raised in Fort Wayne, was a grade school teacher at the time. Dad was a Cleveland, Ohio native, a Navy veteran of the Korean War. He had gone back to school to complete his college degree. As fate would have it, the school he chose was Indiana Tech located in Fort Wayne. Within a year of meeting, they were married, and children quickly followed. As the family grew, dad's career moved us from Indiana to Tampa, Florida to Kansas City. Kansas City was where mom and dad set down roots. It would be our family's last stop, the place where our family memories would be made.

We lived the great middle-America family ideal. The early years of my Oak Street life were like a recipe that mixed together the old TV shows "Leave It To Beaver" and "The Wonder Years," with a Norman Rockwell painting stirred in for good measure. Our family life was the '50s generation's ideal, while living in the '60s. We were untouched by, and only vaguely aware of, the turbulence of that decade. We moved into a brand new two-story house with a two-car garage on a new block in a new suburb of Kansas City, Missouri. It was a place where streets were named after trees and neighbors brought over cakes and cookies and welcomed you to the neighborhood, welcomed you to decades-long friendships. Young couples moved in to raise their kids and stayed long enough to become grandparents.

Our backyard and our neighbors' yards were, by neighborly agreement, not to be fenced. Our shared yards formed a fantastic year-round playing field for football, baseball, kickball, croquet – you name it. If the game involved a ball, we played it. My buddies and I even named our field "Bickertty Stadium" after a conglomeration of our last names. There was lots of blood, sweat and tears spilt on that backyard field, but it was youthful joy and happiness that ruled the day.

Growing up as a kid, my friends and I spent the long days of summer outdoors playing ball or riding our bikes throughout the neighborhood. We rode up to the local shopping center where we visited our favorite store, The Ben Franklin 5 &10, to buy penny candy and baseball cards. Doors were not locked during the day, and mom didn't seem to get particularly worried when we would be gone for hours at a time. On those languid, dog days of summer afternoons simmering with oppressive heat and humidity, we drank lemonade in Dixie cups and played for hours board games like "Risk" and "Monopoly" in the tree shade on our patio. Summer nights were all about the rhythmic buzz of the locusts, flashlight tag and catching lightning bugs.

It was a time when a kid's summer vacation from school lasted for what seemed like an eternity (especially if you were a mom). School was over by Memorial Day, and didn't start back up until after Labor Day. We knew summer was officially over and fall was coming fast when we once again heard that familiar school bell ring. During the school year, we walked to the nearby Catholic grade school and often raced home for lunch and a hug from mom. I raced through lunch so I could get back in time to play "kill the guy with the ball" during recess. This particular game was similar to what you see during a rugby match, only played on our school's asphalt parking lot.

Winters meant waking up to a freezing cold bedroom in the morning, getting up while it was still dark outside, dressing quickly and trudging to church in all manner of weather to serve as an altar boy at the daily early mass. When the first snowfall came, we were out the door to see who could sled the fastest or farthest, or who could get airborne. If the snow was particularly good, we would stack ourselves up on our Flexible Flyer like so much cordwood, push off down our backyard hill and see if this was the time we could make it all the way down the hill without the riders on top falling off.

After the sledding, snowman-building, snow angels and the obligatory snowball fight, one of us would inevitably feel the cold, or get hurt, or take exception to that last of the many snowballs thrown in their face and head inside. When one surrendered, we all surrendered. In we'd troop, shedding sodden gloves and wool hats, snowsuits and black rubber galoshes with those buckles you'd have to strain to snap into place.

And yes, snow days meant drinking mom's hot chocolate made with whole milk and Nestle's Quik, heated up on the stove, and served with marshmallows.

No matter what the season, when dad came home from work, it was our habit to stop whatever we were doing ("Time-out!"), and meet him at the door with a hug and kiss. Greetings exchanged, we'd run off to continue playing ("Time-In!") before being called in for supper. Dad would fix himself a drink, and he and mom would talk about their day while mom fixed dinner in the kitchen. Dinner was called "supper" back then, and sitting down to mom's home-cooked meals to eat together was standard operating procedure for us. No modern-day eating in shifts, no buffet, no fast food and no dining out. We were a stay-at-home family. We knew no other way.

We were not an especially loud or what I would call a boisterous family. My parents were not screamers. They never yelled at each other, and only raised their voices when the kids got out of hand. When they were mad at us, punishment was swift. Mom would get the hairbrush out and swat our rear end or dad would spank us to end and forget the offending incident. "Time out" and "Grounded" had not entered society's lexicon yet; we were simply sent to our rooms where we waited for mom's baking timer to ding and release us from captivity. If things had gone particularly awry for us, we had to wait for dad to come home from work and pronounce further punishment. More often than not though, we were good kids growing up. The sound of children's laughter was not unusual to hear in our house, and we loved to hear our parents laugh. We respected our elders, and dared not talk back to our parents. Yes, there was love in our Oak Street home, but the world also saw a family that was well-mannered, well-groomed and well-provided for.

My father had built a successful career for himself as an executive for a diesel engine company. Dad was his generation's very definition of "the man of the house." He was the breadwinner; seeing to his family's financial well-being was primary. The kids, along with the cooking and cleaning, were mom's day-to-day responsibility. When dad was home, there was never any doubt the chain of command started with him. In an age when parenting evoked a healthy dose of fear in your children, dad was the parent to be feared. It was a time when parents were not expected to play with or entertain their kids. Our parents were not our friends. No, for the most part it was up to us to find our own friends or play together and make our own fun. We never heard of such things as theatre, sports or cheerleading camps to make sure we stayed busy or got the proper amount of exercise.

Our parents did not rely on technology to entertain us either. The TV, still considered a luxury at the time, and not a necessity, was never on during the day, and rarely on at night. Back in the day, there were only three broadcasting channels and no remote control. Watching TV was considered a treat, and shows were strictly monitored by mom. Computers? Nintendo? Ipods? Cell phones? Never heard of them. Can you say rotary-dial phone? The Oak Street early years not only included rotary phones, but phone numbers beginning with letters, as in wi2-1234 for example, the "wi" being short for "willow."

While phone technology improved as we moved into the '70's decade (push button phones!) and into our teenage years, we still remained tethered to the kitchen phone to conduct our embarrassing phone conversations in front of the family. Sometimes we managed to stretch the phone cord to the basement steps around the corner where we gained some measure of privacy by closing the basement door to prying ears. Yeah, I know, I know, by now you get the picture. My little nostalgic look back has confirmed what you already suspected; I'm an old fart. Enough said, let's move on before I'm tempted to tell you about LP's and 8-track tapes.

Fifteen year-old Ace awoke suddenly and sat up. It was another one of those damnable dreams. This time it was the version where dad's plane crashes. Looking out his window's frosted panes, Ace saw the winter night at its darkest and coldest hour. The lone street light showed a sprinkling of snowflakes looking for all the world like salt shaken from a giant salt shaker by God Himself on High. The house was still. The hum of our refrigerator and the lonely whistle of a distant train were all he heard. Everyone was a sleep, his brother and sisters in their rooms and mom in his parents' bedroom. Dad was gone on business again. Ace lay there buried under his blankets and was comforted by the quiet of a peaceful, happy home. He soon went back to a tranquil sleep. Perhaps these dreams were God's benevolent way of preparing his child for the day when his fears became a reality.

Shortly after I turned 16 years old, my troubling dreams stopped. I didn't out grow them; they simply came true. My father's sudden death was not caused by a fiery crash but by the betrayal of his own heart. On a Saturday night in early May of 1974, mom and dad decided to go out and see the current hit movie "The Sting." I was feeling under the weather with a bad cold and stayed home with the rest of the kids. I called it an early night and went to bed before my parents came home. On a Cinco de Mayo Sunday morning, I woke to mom entering my room, sitting down on my bed and softly, sadly, so very sadly, telling me dad had died. I saw mom's utter devastation, and I knew that any pain I felt would never approach the depth of hurt inflicted upon my mother. I felt that if I cried I would only make things worse for her. But the situation called for tears dammit. I'm sure mom's expectation was that I would cry upon hearing the news, and so I did my best imitation of what I thought was an appropriate amount of crying. *We've all been confronted with those occasions when we knew not what to say. When it was painfully obvious the depth of any words of comfort we could offer were no match for the depth of sorrow displayed before us.*

I lay there in bed as the morning light of a beautiful spring day poured through my window. Unexpectedly unsure of his world, unsure if this wasn't just a new version of his bad dreams, doubting Thomas made himself listen as his mother made her death-notice pilgrimage to his sibling's rooms. I lay there, mind and heart numb in disbelief, as I heard the cries of shock and sorrow as one by one they learned of the sudden tragedy that had befallen our now broken all-American family. Perhaps those cursed dreams of mine had after all, in some twisted way, prepared me for this day, the day my dad died of a heart attack at the age of 42. I know the safe, insular world of "Ace" died that day, and those now-prophetic dreams of his as well.

Chapter 2

Amazing Grace

"I once was lost,
But now am found, was blind but now I see.

'Twas grace that taught my heart to fear,
And grace my fears relieved…

'Tis grace has brought me safe thus far,
And grace will lead me home."

Written by John Newton

"Oh my baby, when you're older
Maybe then you'll understand
You have angels to dance around your shoulders
'Cause at times in life you'll need a helping hand

Worry not my daughters
Worry not my sons
Child, when life don't seem worth living
Come to Jesus
And let Him hold you in His arms"

From the song "Come To Jesus"
By Mindy Smith

A Funeral March and Selective Memory

I was raised in the Catholic faith. Both my mother and father were devout Catholics. Dad participated in the liturgy of our faith as a Lector and Cantor, which was pretty cool when I was younger and didn't know better. However, the Cantor gig in particular became decidedly uncool as I entered my self-aware teenage years and watched in amazement as dad stood in front of the whole congregation leading us in song. Truth be told, I was left somewhat embarrassed for him and me. Not because he had a lousy voice, far from it, but because it didn't fit with my image of him as being a man's man kind of guy. Sure, dad would sometimes sit down at the piano in the evenings, pipe firmly clenched in teeth, and play "Born Free" or "The Green, Green Grass of Home." At least that was in the privacy of our own home. To get up in public and sing? Well, that just plain disagreed with my teenage sensibilities of "cool."

Prayer was as much a part of our day as getting dressed in the morning. It was our habit to recite a thanksgiving prayer before and after every meal. When we were young, we said evening prayers together before going off to bed. I recall one evening in particular when our family knelt in the family room while facing the Sacred Heart of Jesus statue prominently displayed on our fireplace mantel. Dad led us in the "Our Father," but stopped us after every stanza and talked about its meaning. It must have taken a half-hour to get through that "Our Father" while us kids, fidgeting on our knees, silently wondered why dad was making such a big deal about a prayer we had learned before we could read.

So it did not come as any surprise on that fateful May 5th Sunday that mom felt it important to fulfill our Sunday obligation and attend mass. Although, we were going to do things a little bit different this time. Attending mass at our church where everyone knew us would be unbearable and was simply out of the question. Mom took us to mass at another Catholic church close by. I remember going through the familiar rituals of mass in that unfamiliar church amongst a congregation of strangers and thinking, "Are these people wondering who we are and why we're here? How obvious is it that we just lost a father and a husband? Could they tell?"

My prayers were by rote; let's just get through this thing was my mindset. I was not there to ask Jesus to welcome dad into His kingdom. I was not there to ask the God of our faith why He had taken my father from me. Somewhat disoriented by what was happening to us, that question would be waiting for me at a later date, but right then I was simply fulfilling my Sunday obligation and my mother's wishes, nothing more.

There are memories of this time, such as us going to mass, that I will never forget. These singular moments in the aftermath of my dad's passing are like scenes in a long-running play acted out on stage while I sit watching from my seat, mesmerized and alone in the darkened theatre. There are also deep fissures in my recollections that have never been filled in or healed for fear of upsetting mom or letting my guard down and exposing myself to additional painful memories I have long hidden away. And while time may heal all wounds, as the saying goes, I may have let too much time go by for those memories I chose to bury, or refused to acknowledge, to come to light and serve any purpose. This is not news to my Oak Street family who knows my memories of events during that time, and subsequent days, months, even years, are blurred like a badly taken picture. On May 5th, 1974 I checked out emotionally as survival mechanism 101.

I do remember calling the priest residence of the Jesuit high school I was attending and telling the unlucky priest who answered that I would not be going to school on Monday on account of my dad having just died. The priest, stammering at this unexpected news delivered as if I was our local TV news anchor reading from the teleprompter, recovered from his surprise, and managed to convey his heart-felt condolences. Somewhat taken aback by the priest's compassionate reaction, I mumbled thanks and quickly hung up. My detached feelings rang hollow in comparison. I was left wondering what was wrong with me.

What I don't remember, and still don't know, is whether it was mom or someone else at the hospital who called our parish priest and asked him to go to the hospital and give my dad his last rites. I don't remember mom making the dreadful phone calls to our extended family and informing them of the terrible news. Who did she call first? How many calls did she have to make and repeat the same anguished story? How the hell did she get through that?

We kids did our best to keep a low profile, to be invisible and hide from our unwanted novelty and the prying eyes of the well-intentioned folks who came to our door. I remember all of us cleaning and re-arranging old furniture and boxes of discarded stuff while taking refuge in the basement. It was a group effort performed with a cooperation, a sense of togetherness, even tenderness, that would rarely be shared by us after that day. Then to, I don't remember ever asking my siblings during that time how they were doing or how they felt about what had happened to them, to us. I don't remember many tears on their part or any attempts on my part to console them. We all seemed to be affected with the same "detachment" malady. I guess we were soldiering on.

What were my dad's last words? Was mom in the ER with dad when he breathed his last breath? Did dad know he was in serious trouble or that he might die? Did he fight for his life knowing what his death would do to mom and our family? How did mom get home from the hospital? Did she drive herself home? Who helped mom with the funeral arrangements? The freaking funeral arrangements, which have got to be the worst, most grotesque shopping experience there is: "Mrs. Bickimer, here is our fine selection of caskets…" I could not ask those questions to mom then, and to this day I never have. I wanted no part in aiding and abetting the pain my shattered mother suffered.

This brings me to a grieving family's first public display of mourning. Let me just say, I'm a little uneasy about the custom of wakes. You have the mourning family there, sitting or standing in front of the casket, greeting and thanking people for coming to their particular rendition of the dramatic play "A Death In Our Family." What are you supposed to say to these sad, well-mannered people trying to hide their sadness and acting the part of the perfect welcoming hosts? Why do they have to be put through this torture with an attempted smile plastered on their faces? Ok, I know not all wakes are, or have to be, this way. But they sure as hell are for the sudden death, the so much to live for and the too young to die.

Somehow, either my father had the remarkable foresight or mom the protective instinct to know how wrenching an open to the public wake would be. Dad's wake became a family-only affair. We would not be put on public display quite yet; the funeral service would be here soon enough. Needless to say, there's not much I remember about my father's wake, other than the distinct funeral home creepy feeling I'd rather be anywhere but there. I absolutely did not want to be anywhere near my father's open casket where a very poor likeness of him lay. That was not how my dad looked or how I wanted to remember him looking.

I took no solace from the funeral service and have little recollection of it. Was my father's favorite hymn "Amazing Grace" played? Was our priest's eulogy for my father personal and anecdotal? Did he tell a compelling story that portrayed the depth and true measure of the man? Did the priest's words comfort us, and somehow offer us hope? Did he comment about the savage unfairness of it all? Did he try to explain how God could be a compassionate and loving God and yet still allow this to happen? I don't remember. What I do remember experiencing is a vague sense of pride for my father upon seeing so many people at the funeral. They were evidence there was a greater world beyond our Oak Street family who had loved and admired him, who must have thought he was a great guy. I took some comfort in that.

A funeral memory that stays with me was what my regrettable interpretation of my newly bestowed title, "the man of the house" was supposed to mean. I thought this meant I was entitled to woodenly stand by mom, distant and unemotional, but in a caring sort of way, all the while pushing my brother out of the way. My little brother, who so very much wanted and needed to be by his mom, and perhaps show he too could be a man of the house. A close friend of mine who attended the funeral would later remark to me how he was touched by the scene at the end of the funeral mass when our family stood at the back of church facing the coffin while the priest said his final prayers, and me standing there next to mom with my arm around her shoulders. It would have made for a touching Hallmark card kind of moment in my memory if not for the fact that it's tinged with the remorse of a big brother who realized too late that he had not yet learned or even knew how to begin to be "the man of the house."

I remember the quiet, insular ride in that long black limousine from the church to the cemetery. Looking out the car's window, I saw that the world looked like any other day. Its sameness jarring compared with the scripted drama being played out by my family and me that day. The bystanders of our funeral march would go back to the normalcy of their daily lives, while we faced the uncertainty of a world forever changed. We had become strangers in a world we once knew and counted on. How I yearned for that departed world. Buck O'Neil, the great Monarchs player and coach from the old Negro Baseball League, once said, "Funerals were for people who died too young. Everyone else deserves a celebration." How right he was, and how right we were to mourn in our funeral black.

I remember sitting in our family room after we came back from the cemetery, graveside rites and public good-byes completed, and eagerly listening to my Uncle Jerry, dad's youngest brother, recount stories of my father's youth. They were wonderful stories I had never heard before, stories that helped color and clarify my picture of a man I knew primarily as performing in the role of my father. We had no family in Kansas City. I don't really remember who all from my mother and father's families came in town to attend the funeral. I don't know when and how they got there or where they stayed. But I will always remember the gift of those stories, and be ever appreciative to my uncle for telling them.

My family's longest day, our funeral march, finally came to an end. The house was emptied of all inhabitants save its founding residents, minus one, who retreated to their respective rooms, where behind closed doors they were left alone with their own thoughts and emotions and, yes, memories to deal with as best they could in the gloom of a most silent night. And lastly, I remember how an exhausted and spent Ace-no-more cried himself to sleep.

Chapter 3

"I'll have a blue Christmas without you.
I'll be so blue just thinking about you."

From the song "Blue Christmas"
By Elvis Presley

Holiday Hell

Mother's Day arrived shortly after my father left. It occurred to us, albeit rather late in the game, that maybe we could cheer mom up if we all chipped in and got her a little something. After all, this was supposed to be a happy occasion. It was the perfect excuse to break out the smiles and ignore our heavy hearts. At the very least we'd pretend there was nothing more important on this day than celebrating mom. We piled into the station wagon, and with me at the wheel headed to the local nursery to buy some flowers. After pooling our money, which must have totaled all of about $12, we managed to make some selections. Choices were limited; the flowers had pretty much been picked over by then, but we're not talking master gardeners here, so it really wouldn't have made much of a difference anyway. After careful horticultural deliberation (How about this one? I don't know, what about this one? I guess. Whatever. At least it's not all wilty and everything.), we came to a consensus on the selections, paid for them, and triumphantly headed home. It was quite the production for a handful of flowers.

There were five of us on that last-minute Mother's Day shopping run. I had three sisters, ages 15, 13, and 8, and my brother was 12. At 16, I was the oldest of the brood. All in all, I'd say we had gotten along pretty well with each other as kids growing up. We played together quite a bit, and as long as everyone did what I wanted to do, well, at least I was happy. Besides, we knew if we started arguing with each other, or if things got too out of hand, punishment would be parentally swift. Then the teenage years arrived. The teen years were changing the group dynamics that's for sure, and while I think we were still pretty civil with each other, there were times when we barely tolerated each other. The higher the hormonal levels rose, the fewer the activities we did as a group and the more we wanted to be left alone. If you want to, go to the end of Chapter 7 for a better understanding of what I'm talking about here.

Yet, there we were, out shopping together, united in heart-felt appreciation for mom. Into the house we trooped, happy and pleased with ourselves, and presented her with the flowers there in the kitchen where she was fixing dinner. I don't know if it was the sorry state of the flowers - they were a little on the wilted side - or the sorry state of our family's well-being, but with the best of intentions we caused the one thing we were united against to happen: we made mom cry.

With the appearance of those tears, the smiles on our faces disappeared, and with a sinking heart I began to realize we were up against something that could not be easily dismissed. I had hoped that, any time now, mom's grief and our grief would soon just disappear. I kind of thought it was like having the chicken pox or mumps. You're sick a week, two weeks tops, and then you feel better. A little scarring perhaps, but other-wise everything is back to normal. I guess you could call this one of those teachable moments we all have, one of those hard lessons we'd rather not have to learn.

Must I mention that first Father's Day after dad's death? Boy, how I dreaded that approaching day. Suffice it to say I felt like an alien from another planet when it finally did arrive. Our family's unspoken strategy was simply to do our best to ignore the day's celebration. We were determined to be as inconspicuous as possible and treat it like we would any other day. This would be the first test of the depth of all of our self-pity. We huddled in our house and avoided the well-intentioned outside world's prying eyes curious about the coping skills of this fatherless family. But shit, the one thing we could not hide from was our festering grief. For me, the day exposed my false confidence that I had things under control. By the end of the day, I was left with the sorry feeling that I had miserably failed this pity test. I hated that day for the way it made me feel and for what it had put my family and me through. I hated being me that day.

Later in the year, having gotten a little taste of what was in store for us, a feeling of dread slowly began to squeeze my insides as the big holidays of Thanksgiving and Christmas approached. They would have the dubious distinction of being the first Thanksgiving and first Christmas after my father's death. No question about it, these were going to be holidays to survive, not celebrate. They served as not so subtle reminders that our lives were a precarious balancing act of ragged emotions. Yes, we would get through them, but all these damn holidays, whether it was Thanksgiving, Christmas or the freaking Fourth of July, really screwed with our fragilely constructed picture of what it meant to be a normal family. There would be little happiness on these days. There was only a muted sadness, a faux happiness dressed up with brave, smiling faces. Did we really have to celebrate them? What was the point?

Mom thought we should try to escape the ghosts of happy Thanksgivings past and the trials of a Thanksgiving present by packing up and leaving town. We spent the holiday at a summer resort located at the Lake of the Ozarks. Now, I'm sure this is a great place to visit in June or July, what with the lake and pool and all. But the frost had long since been on the pumpkin, and the cold, damp, grey weather lent an air of abandonment to a place that was already as quiet as a church. Mom's diversion tactic, made with the best of intentions, went miserably awry. Our isolation and loneliness were painfully evident as we half-heartedly ate our institutional turkey dinner in the deserted resort restaurant. Dinner could not end fast enough. The words "sullen" and "somber" come to mind as just the right adjectives to describe a scene nobody, but nobody, wanted to be a part of. Our great escape had failed. We couldn't get home fast enough. Happy Freaking Thanksgiving. Only 26 long shopping days left till Christmas!

Let's just say there were no Kodak moments during that "first" Christmas. The Madison Avenue version of "happy holidays" is rarely what its cracked up to be, even in the best of times. As it is for many people at this time of year, I recall feeling an all too familiar loneliness and isolation. As I've mentioned, there was no extended family in town to gather with, which was probably just as well because I had no desire to be the object of anybody's sympathy anyway. Besides, our most loyal visitors at this time of year, our grandparents, would not be coming. There would be no Christmas packages and tinned homemade cookies to unload from the trunk of grandpa's car. There would be no grandma.

Just for good measure, let's turn the misery level up another notch with the sudden death of my grandmother, my mom's mom. Unsettled by how this could be happening to us, I remember thinking, well shit, who's next? Shortly after Thanksgiving, we made the funeral march up to Fort Wayne for another long good-bye. Mom was abandoned once again, and we kids got to miss a couple of days of school as a consolation prize for reliving our own not too distant feelings of abandonment.

Bernadette and Harold. Grandma and grandpa. She a devout Catholic, he a staunch Lutheran. Both set in their ways, they always seemed to be on each other's nerves. We loved seeing them though, whether it was when they visited us during the holidays or we came to them during our family's summer vacation. The car trip to their home in Fort Wayne was half our visit's fun. The backseat of our brown, imitation wood-paneled station wagon was folded down so all five kids could stretch out with our pillows and read, play games like "Twenty Questions" or compare the small treasures and treats found in the brown paper goody bags mom made-up for each of us.

I can still see my grandparent's one-story home on Riverside Drive: the native Indiana limestone on the front of the house, the yard shaded by giant trees and the sunny guest bedroom with hardwood floors and a big four-poster bed we loved to climb up on. When we arrived, one of the first things I noticed was their house had a different smell to it than our house did. It was a nice smell. It evoked a sense of comfort and security, correctness and order. Even as a young boy, I recognized the left over ambiance of a by-gone era. Grandma, wearing her house dress and apron, was the undisputed master of her kitchen. We could always find her there cooking or sewing, ready with a kind word, a soft touch for a mid-afternoon snack. Grandpa, uniformed in dark brown slacks and a button-down shirt, was a bit gruff but always kind. He was A-Ok in my book because he occasionally took me golfing and let me push around the yard a really cool vintage reel lawn mower. He played the organ that dominated their living room, and was a soap opera watcher who was never to be disturbed during the afternoon hour when his favorite program "As The World Turns" was on.

I killed my first chipmunk during one of our visits to grandma and grandpa's. We often played baseball in the back yard with a whiffle ball and a big, red, plastic bat. One afternoon I was retrieving the ball from grandpa's garden, big bat in hand, and happened across a chipmunk. He (She? It?) had to have been the world's dumbest, slowest and on that day, unluckiest chipmunk. He was the lone exception to Darwin's theory of survival of the fittest. I don't know what came over me, but I took that big red bat and....whap! He was my first and last chipmunk kill. I had just proved Darwin's theory was still applicable in nature, but for a long time afterwards I carried with me a guilty conscious for what I had done to poor Alvin.

Fond memories, but I seem to have veered off course a little bit. Let's get back to a less happier time shall we? As we returned home from Fort Wayne, I imagined hearing the unmistakable sound of a door slamming shut on the last vestiges of that by-gone era known as my boyhood.

What an effort it was to summon enough Yuletide energy to decorate the tree that year. How subdued it seemed as we gathered together Christmas Eve to exchange presents while the Ray Conniff Singers sang "Deck the Halls" and "We Wish You A Merry Christmas." How surreal it was for me to dress up as Santa for our neighbors next door. But sure enough, there I was, bearded, pillowed and itchy in my red suit as I trudged across the snowy yard with all kinds of Christmas cheer running through my head (that's a little sarcasm there). I rang the doorbell. The door was thrown open, and I remember being blasted by the resounding joy and happiness of our neighbor's Christmas party. There must have been a hundred family members there. How the hell did I let myself get talked into this deal? Was I out of my mind? Sweating profusely under my suit, I passed out their goodies, HoHoHo'd in my squeaky teen voice and got the hell out of there as fast as I could. Safely back home, and much to my relief, mom stayed put with all of us. There was no attempted out-of-town escape, and we managed to make it through the rest of a season's glad tidings and good cheer without further injury or additional trauma.

Finally, the worst year of our lives came staggering to a close. I think it would be safe to say that New Year's Eve was greeted not with a celebration of a year gone by and the anticipation of a new year to come, but with an exhausted sigh of relief. We longed for life to be better than the nightmare we had just endured. Though, I for one gave it the ol' college try and tried to get into the New Year's Eve festivities. Leaving mom and siblings to their own devices, I took off with some friends and headed for a classmate's annual New Year's Eve bash. There were no parents to be seen. The house was stuffed to the rafters with kids, there were kegs on ice and classic rock music of the '70s like "Sweet Home Alabama" was cranked up. What could be better than this, right? Have you ever had this weird experience where you're at a party or a large gathering of some sort, everything and everyone is amped-up, and suddenly you feel unconnected from it all? It's almost like you're invisible. That's what happened to me. I don't know whether it was sensory overload or alcohol overload, but whatever it was I didn't last long. Just like the year we were saying good riddance to, I staggered home and crawled into bed before the last musical strains of "Auld Lang Syne" were heard.

Years later as I attempt to tell this story while struggling to dredge up long-buried memories, I wonder if during that holiday season of 1974 we glimpsed a glimmer of hope that is Christ's birth celebrated at Christmas time. I suppose that would just be revisionist history on my part. I guess that pitfall comes with the retelling. It's difficult to resist the temptation to magically recall a difficult time with a positive spin, to catch yourself wishing to believe or to remember that some of us were looking forward to a rebirth of our own selves, as we each in our own way and time struggled to come to terms with the death of our old selves. The fact is we were teenagers, kids after all. I know there were none of these existential, philosophical, feel-good thoughts rattling around in my brain at the time. No, I just knew the whole scene sucked.

Chapter 4

"Hear his song in rainy days,
gridiron games, rolling fairways.
Hear his song in the new generation voices,
in our holy contemplative choices."

From "Brian's Song"
by T.J.B.

"Oh very young
What will you leave us this time?
You're only dancing on this earth for a short while
Oh very young
What will you leave us this time?"

From the song "Oh Very Young"
By Cat Stevens

Sports Stories and A Word About Cemetery Visits

On my 13th or 14th birthday, I forget which, I was given a basketball goal and pole for my birthday present. That was the good news. The bad news was there were strings attached with the gift. I would have to be the one who dug the hole next to our driveway for the pole to stand in. I was pretty excited about getting the basketball goal, and at first, the thought of digging a 3-foot hole in the ground didn't seem like such a big deal, it might even be fun. A couple of hours of hard labor, a half-day tops, and I would soon be shooting hoops in my driveway.

Now, my birthday is in March, and March in Kansas City during my early years was in the pre-climate-change era when it was still pretty damn cold and not that unusual to see snow on the ground. In other words, I found out pretty quickly that digging frozen ground was not as easy a task as first thought. My initial enthusiasm and excitement turned to grim labor as each day after school I fought my way down through the frozen tundra. Hours turned into days, but with blistered hands and dogged determination I finally got the hole dug. Maybe it wasn't all the way down to the recommended three feet, but close enough.

Once that goal was raised, there was a lot of basketball played on the driveway over the years. At all times of day and in all kinds of weather, I would be out by myself or with others playing "Around the world," "Horse," or pick-up games where you called your own fouls and baskets were kept track of by ones. There were times to, when we would be playing and dad would come home from work and shoot around with us for a couple of minutes before going inside to greet mom. I remember the last couple of times dad stepped onto the "court" and fired his old-school set-shot. He would grab his arm with a grimace and mutter something about getting old. Looking back, was this one of those early warning signs for heart attacks you hear about?

The basketball goal story is pretty typical of how dad operated as a father. Although we knew he cared for us, dad was not a play with your kids, teach-them-to-play kind of guy. He pretty much left it up to me to develop an interest in a sport, and my interest in sports coincided with my friends' interest in sports. If I wanted to keep my friends, I had better learn how to catch, throw, or shoot a ball. It was up to me to figure out the how-to's. Sports camps were not in the family budget, self-taught was. I was not given the sports equipment on demand either, as if it was some sort of birthright. I had to make do with whatever I could scrounge up on my own or wait until my birthday or Christmas rolled around. When those times came, dad made sure I was properly equipped, and every once in awhile he would shoot some baskets with me or play catch in the backyard.

As I got older, I became more cunning, at least in my estimation, about equipping myself for the next sports season. One year I contrived to convince mom to help me pay for a baseball glove to give as a present to dad on his birthday in

February. Spring training hadn't even started, but there was no doubt about it, dad needed a new ball glove, and the new Denny McLain model was just the one for him. Never mind that it would come with the rights to borrow it from him whenever I needed it. Never mind that dad conveniently let me take care of it when he wasn't using it.

Another sports-related memory I have is going to a late season, night ballgame with dad at old Memorial Stadium where the Kansas City A's played. It was the first baseball game I ever went to, and what's more, I got to watch the young pitching phenom Vida Blue perform before a large crowd charged with excitement and anticipation. At that time, the A's were not very good, but they were a young up-and-coming team that would soon be a baseball dynasty (albeit in Oakland, the city where their infamous owner, Charlie Finley, moved the team). Vida Blue, the rookie pitcher who was having a sensational year, was the embodiment of his team's talent and promise. I don't remember who won the game, but I do vividly remember a boy no older than 10 sitting next to his dad in the shadows of a stadium-lit, cool September evening. He was soaking in the excitement of the game, the crowd and the aura of a special life event.

As I grew older and my relationship with my father grew more complicated by our rapidly diverging opinions and lifestyles, there remained the cross-generational, common denominator of sports that bonded father and son. In particular, we shared a love for the game of golf, and it became a subject we could always count on having a safe conversation. I guess you could say if Dad had a hobby, it was playing golf. He never played on weekends, which would have taken away from family time, but he would play during the week, usually as a way to entertain business clients and potential customers. We scraped together some used clubs and I began to play with some of my neighborhood friends at the nearby municipal course. Through his company, dad became a member of the local country club, which served as the venue for his golf outings. Dad let me join the club's junior golf program as well. I was hooked on the game, and it would become a life-long hobby of mine.

When I started high school, I was too young to get a job at a store or restaurant, but I discovered I was old enough to caddy at the club. I just had to be big enough to carry a member's bag for 18 holes, which is a hike of about 4 miles. I would ride my bike to the club and then wait my turn in the caddy shack for a morning round of 18 holes, or "loop" in caddy parlance. If it was a busy day, I could even get an afternoon loop. It was hard work for a skinny kid who didn't weigh much more than some of the member's bags he hauled around. We were paid in cash, and while it wasn't much, it was great to have a little spending money in my pocket. There was an added perk as well; caddies got to play free on Mondays when the course was closed. Technically, as a member by way of my dad, I could play at the club whenever I wanted. But other than the occasional junior golf day, I didn't. Dad treated the club membership as more of a business expense than a family privilege, so the best opportunity for me to play golf became those Monday afternoons when caddies played for as long as they wanted.

Caddying was my first job. It was also my first step beyond the innocence of the world I grew up in. Among other things, this new world taught me how to cuss like a sailor and smoke like James Dean. I was introduced to a different way of looking at girls and not necessarily in a nice way. In this country club world I learned about capitalism, which golfers tipped the best and who bought you lunch at the turn. If you provided the best service, you were in demand and got the best loops. I learned some things about gambling and poor sportsmanship. It didn't take long to find out which golfers threw clubs or stiffed you with no tip if they lost their bet. I saw that success on and off the course often followed those golfers who were considerate and thoughtful towards me. I recall a guy named Wilbur who I often caddied for. He was a one-eyed golfer who also happened to be the club champion. He showed me you could overcome handicaps and still excel.

My caddy master introduced me to dirty books, which he read an abundance of. He often quoted passages to either gross us out or make us (me) turn red with embarrassment. I remember him taking particular delight in a book called "The Exorcist." And I was taught, no, made to play a game called "Bloody Knuckles." To pass the time between loops, caddies would gather in the caddy shack and play this game where you and your opponent would begin by touching fist to fist, and then one would try to rap the other on top of the knuckles first. If you lost, you had to place your hand flat on the table, and the winner could then smash his fist down on your hand. To be fair, the rule was the winner could not raise his fist above his head, but it still hurt like hell if it was your hand on the table. All in all, besides the occasional swollen hand, I was discovering what a grand variety of human beings there were in the world. And there I was, a willing student, learning the ways of the country club set and the caddy shack set while trying to figure out just where the hell I fit in with these parallel universes.

I took pride in my first real job, and became pretty good at it too. There came a day when dad asked me if I wanted to caddy for him. There weren't many opportunities to be with him outside the usual family environment. Man, I was excited to show him how good a caddy I was, and to show him how grown-up I was becoming. It was a fun afternoon. I loved being with dad, watching him play, and listening to him as he bantered with his business associates. He and his friends included me in their fun, and I basked in the obvious pride my father took in me. Dad worked hard, he travelled a lot and put in long hours. This was how he relaxed, and I reveled in his happiness. Sometime during that golf round dad declared, "You've got to take time to smell the roses!" I think he was saying this as much for his own benefit as he was for his friends or me. In retrospect, my father didn't get enough time to smell the roses.

Mom was never one to push a visit to the cemetery on us. I don't remember her ever asking me to go with her to the cemetery, and I never asked her if she would like to go. I was afraid of burdening mom with the sadness I knew would accompany our visit to dad's gravesite. Perhaps mom felt the same way about taking us as well. I know of families who bring their lawn chairs and picnic at their loved one's gravesite. Our family was not like that. We could not celebrate a beloved's long and prosperous life. We could only mourn the loss of a life ended way too soon. Why put ourselves through more misery by going to the cemetery? I know it's a little weird, but I taught one of my sisters how to drive on the roads of that cemetery, and never once did we stop and visit our father's grave.

I'm reminded of my father's younger brother who would come from out-of-town and pay us an occasional visit. Usually it was during times when one of us had a graduation or significant birthday. My Uncle David, a wonderful, gifted man, a professor of education and a man of letters and music, inevitably insisted we all take a trip to the cemetery. I could understand why my uncle wanted to visit his brother's gravesite, but it seemed pretty insensitive and disconcerting as hell to drag us along as well. I mean, come on! Happy freaking birthday! Let's go to the cemetery! I never understood why he insisted we make those visits with him. It was almost as if he took comfort in the safety of our numbers, gloomily standing there next to him, as he came face to face with his own conflicted memories of another time shared with his older brother.

It was the same old story of well-intentioned folks failing to understand our feelings by projecting what they thought we should be feeling onto us. How we chose to deal with such a catastrophic loss in our lives was a personal journey each of us undertook in our own unique way. The distance traveled was not the same, and for some of us, the journey was longer and harder to navigate than it was for others. Again that old adage, "Time heals all wounds," comes to mind. The concept of time becomes relative here, doesn't it? One person's time to heal can be blessedly short, while another's could take a lifetime. You may eat together as a family or even pray together, but that doesn't necessarily mean you heal together as a family. Do you wait for each other, or do you push on? Do they wait for you? Does one ever really completely heal from such a painful experience, or does that person simply find it easier to get on with life by nurturing the memories he chooses to remember and burying the rest? It's like recovering from knee surgery. After surgery you begin your recovery on crutches. Then there is the painful rehabilitation. Some people heal faster than others. You may end up with a slight limp or an occasional ache, and there will always be a scar.

What time has given me is perspective. Maybe it's not exactly healing, but close enough. You know, I continued to caddy and play golf after dad died. The club membership disappeared with dad, but I returned to caddy for awhile. And before I left my caddying career, I took one or two final lessons from there. I learned goodness can be found in whatever world you chose to travel in. The club's assistant pro, Bob, as nice as the head pro was crusty, took time to show particular kindness to me and welcome me back to work after dad died. I came back to the privileged golfers and the caddy shack gang, each with their own version of the game "Bloody Knuckles." It was during this time I found the secret to winning that game: Never let your opponent see your pain, even if time and time again, it was your hand being smashed on the table. If you showed no pain, if you refused to acknowledge that pain no matter how hurt you were, your opponent would eventually tire and make a mistake or get frustrated and quit. I ruled at that game.

I came back for the Monday golf outings as well. Sorry to do this to you, but I can't resist pointing out how I've learned that the game of golf can be a wonderful metaphor for life. It's a thoughtful, quiet game played at the pace you set, in solitude or as a shared pursuit. There is no game clock. The round is over when you are done playing, no matter how long it takes or how well you played. A golfer is rewarded for their ability and skill, but his best shot sometimes might not be good enough when the ball bounces the wrong way. How you play the game, the display of one's honesty and integrity, is more than a cliché. It's truly a valued part of golf.

There is one cemetery visit I remember making on my own when I felt particularly alone and fatherless. I had gone there in an almost desperate attempt to hang on to my fading connection with dad. I stood before his granite-inscribed name and allowed myself to give in to self-pity and the anguish washing over me as I fought the lengthening shadows obscuring my memories of my father. It was a cleansing of sorts, an unburdening of a pain that had become too heavy to carry and too big to hide. I stood there in cemetery quiet, absorbed in holy contemplation, letting the spring sun's warmth fill my emptiness with promise. It's the kind of promise that takes the sting out of lessons learned the hard way, it's a promise of life-lessons still to be learned, and the promise found in memories too brilliant to succumb to the darkest of shadows. In golf, the person farthest away plays first. Before I turned to leave, I placed two golf balls on his grave, one for him and one for me. Play on.

Chapter 5

"I have my books
And my poetry to protect me;
I am shielded in my armor,
Hiding in my room, safe within my womb.
I touch no one and no one touches me.
I am a rock,
I am an island.

And a rock feels no pain;
And an island never cries."

From the song "I Am A Rock"
By Simon & Garfunkel

Wrestling With Demons

After the funeral and last sincere, but not really, "If there is anything we can do for you, be sure to let us know," had left, it was just the six of us again. They returned to their comfortable worlds of order, and we were left to our world-turned-upside down. Having no idea what the protocol was for our current situation, the kids decided to give ourselves a couple more days off before going back to school. It seemed like a good idea to let the novelty of our fatherless selves wear off some before facing friends, classmates and teachers. We soon found out however, those days at home felt like we had been placed under quarantine, and I was getting anxious to escape the cloak of gloom we were living under at home.

Honestly, I didn't know how long I was supposed to feel bad. I didn't know how long we were supposed to share our grief with each other. Just what was the protocol for this kind of thing? How long were we supposed to mourn? When could we smile again? When could we crack jokes and laugh again? Getting back to school appeared to be the best way to get out of the fix we found ourselves in.

I wasn't sure what to expect when we went back, but I was pretty sure I would have to cope with the unwanted attention and special treatment that comes with being the different kid. At first, it was different. It was kind of like walking into a room full of people, and whether you know them or not, everyone turns, surreptitiously or blatantly, to look at you. There's that slight pause in the room's conversations, and you immediately feel self-conscious and uncomfortably self-aware.

Fortunately, those first days back, duck-out-of-water moments were short-lived. Teenagers are pretty good at overlooking the obvious, especially in an all-boys school like mine. My conversations back at school were pretty much along the lines of, "Sorry about your dad." "Thanks." Five seconds of silence, then, "So, do you think the Royals are going to be any good this year?" It didn't take long for everybody to get used to each other again, to fall back on old familiarity and the normal routine of school life. My teachers were great. For the most part I was given a pass on make-up work and accorded a certain amount of latitude with my grades as well. I wasn't one to take advantage of their generosity, but there was no way in hell any of my teachers were going to give me a bad grade after the awful circumstances I had experienced.

I should mention here that this was my second year participating on the high school wrestling team. For the uninitiated, there is nothing pretty about the sport of wrestling. It's a demanding sport where one-on-one matches contribute to a team's success or failure. But teamwork is not part of a wrestler's formula for success. There are no teammates out there on the mat with you to rely on. It was just your bad-ass self against the bad-ass opponent across from you. When I joined the team as a freshman, I was 105 pounds of good sportsmanship and friendly disposition. Unfortunately for me, this was the wrong combination of attributes required to successfully compete in a tough sport like wrestling. There was no doubt about it, I was friggin' horrible. To be fair, I had no previous experience in the sport other than occasionally watching "All-Star Wrestling" when I came across it on late night TV.

Unfortunately again for me, I just happened to be the best of the lot on our team who could wrestle at that skinny-ass weight. As long as I wasn't pinned by my opponent, and that was a 50/50 proposition at best, I was actually helping the team by showing up on the mat and getting my butt whipped. It was purely a scoring strategy on my coach's part. Filling my weight class for our meets, even if it didn't amount to much more than throwing a warm body on the mat, gave fewer points to the other team than if our team had no wrestler at all. My coach looked at it in terms of something was better than nothing. It certainly wasn't better for me, but it was for him.

By some miracle, I lettered in the sport my freshman year. The coach must have felt, one, pity for me, and two, guilty for throwing me to the wolves as our team's sacrificial lamb. Maybe coach thought if he gave me a varsity letter I would take it for what it was: recognition for survival, certainly not for ability or success. Surely I would realize I was in over my head, come to my senses and try another after-school activity that better suited my unique talents, whatever those might be. But paybacks are hell. Coach underestimated my capacity to ignore the obvious and forget the recent past. To his astonishment, I came back my sophomore year.

Anyway, when I returned to school after my dad died, the wrestling season was coming to a close. Things had gone no better for me this year wrestling at the heftier 112 weight class than they had the year before. When I got back, my heart just wasn't into the tough practices and stringent dieting needed to make weight, only to be humiliated again on the mat. But I couldn't quit just yet. I wanted one last chance to redeem myself at our next meet. During my hiatus, I had lost my varsity spot; so I would wrestle JV, where I might actually be competitive, and maybe, just maybe, have a chance to win. I spent the day before and the day of our meet constantly weighing myself as I tried to make weight. You wrestlers know the drill. I barely ate, and ran in heavy sweats up and down an infernal amount of stairs in the school stairwell closest to the wrestling room which was tucked away in a dingy corner of the school's basement. A couple of hours before the meet I finally reached the required weight limit of 112 pounds and was ready to go.

Cue the famous "Wide World of Sports" intro: "The thrill of victory and the agony of defeat." I got out on the mat and wrestled as well as I knew how. I wrestled with determination, fearlessness and with heart. I wrestled for my dad, and for mom who was in the stands that night watching me for the first time. For three periods the match went back and forth between my opponent and me. Two lanky titans of the wrestling mat, possessing marginal skills at best, battling it out. When it was over, the referee did not raise my hand. I had narrowly lost on points. Still, I walked off that mat satisfied I had given it my all. I had made mom proud. Mom, who knew nothing about wrestling, did know something about the human spirit. She recognized my effort for what it was, a validation of my self-esteem.

Although my hand was not raised in victory, there was no "agony of defeat." I proved to myself I was wrestling-worthy. More importantly, I proved to myself that I could be tested and competitively respond with strength of body and character. I had done my best, and I knew dad would have been proud, was proud. Come to think of it, the match would have made for a pretty compelling made-for-TV pro-wrestling script, without the obligatory chair smashed over the head and gallons of spilled blood of course. I chose to see victory in my defeat. By my way of thinking, I accomplished what I had set out to do. Having proven myself without the validation of a varsity letter, I hung up my wrestling shoes and never wrestled again.

Is there ever a good time to die? In the case of my dad's

departure, my God, you've seen our survival numbers. We had one widowed parent and five fatherless children. Three of those kids were teenagers and a fourth soon to be. Talk about bad timing. Talk about being thrown to the wolves. This was a Molotov cocktail of grief-stricken, hormone-raging teenage angst. What would be the coping skills this ex-wrestler could rely on? I was about as prepared to face this challenge as I was as an inexperienced freshman wrestling for the first time in his life. Throw in the drama of an everyday teenager, and can you tell me just how in the ever-loving world this was all supposed to work out?

As the elder son, the oldest child, the newly anointed "man of the house," I chose to navigate our fatherless future by walking a path of least resistance. I pretty much abandoned ship and left my family to fend for themselves. I was the lonely wrestler, knowing after all that there is no "I" in teamwork. I think it would be accurate to say we kids all seemed to retreat to our respective corners, to our individual worlds where we felt most comfortable. After all, we went to different schools, hung out with different friends and had our own gender-specific activities. When our circular, insular worlds intersected at home, home no longer felt like a sanctuary where we could retreat to share the troubles and good times of each other's experiences. Yes, I played the good son as best I could. I lived by the creed that what mom didn't hear, see, or know about shouldn't compound the hurt she was already going through. And yes, I accepted my role as big brother, but the half-hearted effort I gave to that role produced the predictable results of being only a marginally good one.

From my narrow vantage point, my two teenage sisters were doing ok adapting to our circumstances. Besides, they had each other to work out any problems they might be having. When their social worlds happened to collide with mine, I was generally more aloof than welcoming, almost afraid they would bring with them the melancholia of home that I was doing my best to escape from, unaware that perhaps they too were making their own escape. I had little in common with my younger brother. I convinced myself I was too busy to take the time to try and figure out what we could do together. He was having difficulties before dad died, and the truth was, I sure as hell didn't want any part of his world or his troubles now that dad was gone. Mom never asked me to act as a father-figure towards my brother. There were times when she insisted that he looked up to me and to keep that in mind, but my brother and I knew better. I had no clue about my youngest sister. The difference in our ages pretty much assured our experiences would remain worlds apart. Surely my mom or other sisters would take care of her needs. I ignored her, what could a little girl possibly have to worry about or expect from me?

As far as I was concerned, it was everyman for himself, like the wrestler who competes by himself, for himself. Only my opponent would not be the singlet-attired, cauliflower-eared beast I typically had come across on the mat. No, my opponent would be the just as scary inner-demons lurking beneath the impassive surface of my fragile psyche. I didn't want to, or couldn't, take on more than that. So as long as you didn't bother me, I wouldn't bother you, and we would get along just fine. The fatherless man-child became an island. He wrapped himself in a cocoon of self-centeredness and went it alone. It seemed to be the safe thing to do when your heart was broken.

Chapter 6

"Well I know it wasn't you who held me down,
Heaven knows it wasn't you who set me free,
So often times it happens that we live our lives in chains,
And we never even know we have the key."

From the song "Already Gone"
By The Eagles

Drunk On Self-Pity

A cautionary note to all you young adults out there, the legal age for drinking adult beverages was 18 at the time my story takes place. This is not an explanation for the stupidity of some of my actions, but perhaps it helps put into perspective my behavior in a time much different than today. Having proclaimed my disclaimer, let's get back to the story.

On the day I turned 16 years old, I passed my driver's test and was awarded an authentic driver's license from the Missouri Department of Motor Vehicles. There had been a lot riding on me passing that test successfully. Obviously, there were the legalized driving privileges that came with the license, but a date with a girl was at stake as well. Not only a date, but a chance to take this girl to my first school dance the next day. Earlier I had worked up enough courage to ask this girl to the dance, with the small condition of having to pass the driver's test first. The poor girl, and thus her mom, had to wait until the day before the dance to know for sure whether she was even going. You parents can appreciate the tough circumstances I put this girl in, what with all the logistical planning involving dresses, shoes, hair and who knows what all else girls go through to prepare for a dance. Shoot, all I had to worry about was the stupid test, buying something called a "boutonniere" for my date to wear, and getting dad's permission to drive his car that night.

Well, having passed the test with flying colors, I gave her the green light, and dad gave me the go-ahead to use his car for the night. Now because dad's business involved the selling and repairing of diesel truck engines, his company car was a diesel Mercedes sedan. This was a well-earned business perk that by no means reflected our standard of living. Dad could have easily chosen mom's station wagon for me to take, but he didn't, which gets us to the point of my story. I think it tells you a lot about the man. Having gone through parenthood myself, I shake my head in wonder at his psychological genius. Dad was willing to gamble I'd return his car in the same pristine condition it was in when I pulled out of the garage for my date. He put his trust in a wet-behind-the-ears, rookie kid driver.

To raise the stakes even higher, wouldn't you know the night of the dance we experienced one helluva thunderstorm. Dad never flinched. With rain pouring down, thunder and lightning crackling all around, he gave me the car keys with little more than a cautionary "let's be careful out there." I took a big gulp, and away I went. I was scared half to death driving that thing. I may have driven like an 80-year-old grandma that night, but I got his car back home no worse for wear. And my reward? I was given a pretty affectionate kiss by my date at the end of the night. I wasn't sure if it was more out of gratitude for getting her safely home or because she liked me, but I went with the liking me scenario. Looking back as a veteran parent of the teenage wars, I've got to say with all due admiration, what dad did that night was pretty damn impressive.

Shortly thereafter, I proceeded to my next rite of passage: obtaining a not-so-authentic second driver's license. Some friends and I were given what was deemed to be reliable information about how and where this could be accomplished. We drove to a downtown Kansas City location, and under the cover of broad daylight we walked into a photo-developing store that was obviously, at least to our imaginative selves, an elaborate front for their real business, the production of fake driver's licenses. After paying a take-it-or-leave it exorbitant fee, 20 minutes later I walked out with a license proclaiming my birth to be two years earlier than my actual birthday. This was huge! I was 16 years old and looked like I was 12, but I could now walk into any bar, liquor store or (dinosaur alert) disco in the city. As the school year came to a close, the world of 3-2 beer and Boone's Farm wine opened up for me. My friends and I would no longer have to stand outside 7-11 stores soliciting older accomplices to buy beer for us. I could look forward to a summer of a new driver's freedom empowered by a license showing my newly revised age of 18. Hot damn, summer was going to be awesome!

There were, indeed, fun times during that summer of the year of becoming fatherless. We were still a two-car family, and dad's car had been replaced by a fairly new Ford Cougar. A tan two-door model with a 350 engine, it was a pretty cool car for a teenage kid to be tooling around in. Now, I was no motor head. I could change a tire, the car battery, even the oil, but that was the extent of my auto mechanic skills. I also happened to know that if you flipped the carburetor lid over, the intake could suck air in faster allowing me to accelerate quicker. Handy to know when a particularly pesky kid in my class who had the same model of car as mine would challenge me to races down Ward Parkway after school.

With hip transportation and cold adult beverages readily available, I made the most of my opportunities to experience the fruits of my new found freedom. Mom had other things on her mind, and as long as I flew under the radar, there wasn't much concern about parental control cramping my style. Don't worry; I'm not going to start telling a bunch of those-were-the-good-old-days stories of my youth. I'll limit my narrative to one memorable party I attended that summer relevant to what I'm writing about here and that has stayed with me to this day.

I happened to be at a party at the mid-town home of a friend of mine one evening while his parents were conveniently gone. There also happened to be large quantities of beer conveniently available for consumption. At some point during the evening's festivities, I found myself seated in a somewhat comatose state with a young lady perched on my lap. The Eagles' song, "Take It Easy," with the lyrics, "It's a girl, my Lord, in a flatbed Ford slowing down to take a look at me," for some inexplicable reason kept playing on a continuous loop in my sodden brain. I had no idea who she was or how she got there, but if she wanted to take a load off her feet by sitting on my lap, well, fine, that was ok by me. However, at some point she became a little impatient with me, maybe even a little upset that I wasn't paying more attention to her. After all, I was doing a pretty damn good impersonation of an inanimate piece of furniture.

Let me just interject here, that in no way was my inability to interact with the opposite sex in this particular instance indicative of how I acted in a sober state of mind. At any rate, a friend of mine happened to be observing this sorry state of affairs. By way of explanation or apology for me, he told the girl to leave me alone because my father had recently died. Well that pretty much spoiled what little mood there was between her and me. The girl decided to cut her losses. She jumped up and without so much as a good-bye, she was gone, leaving me forlorn and ready to get the hell out of that party as fast as possible.

Here's the deal. When I lost my father, I no longer felt like I was just a normal guy. I had become different than my friends. I was the guy who had the bad luck of having his father die on him. While I felt this made me worthy of other people's sympathy, I certainly didn't want their sympathy or special attention. It became my habit to answer with monosyl-lable responses of "Thanks....Fine....Yeah....Thanks" those who approached me with, "I'm sorry to hear about your dad.... How are you doing?....It must be hard....If there's anything I can do...." All the while me silently screaming, "I don't want to f'n talk about it! There is no way in HELL you could pos-sibly understand what I'm going through!"

My friend took himself away from a raging-good party to drive me home. It was a pretty quiet ride. Up until then, I thought I had done a pretty good job of keeping feeling sorry for myself under wraps. But I had let my guard down and let my self-pity percolate to the surface with this public display of drunkenness. I was ashamed and embarrassed. Wallowing in self-pity would only be tolerated in the loneliness of my own room, preferably during rainy days, or cold, grey winter days to set just the right kind of mood for wretchedness. What's more, I was mortified that I had let this happen with a young lady's affections on the line. My God, what the hell was wrong with me? Stupid, stupid, stupid!

As I got out of his car, I may have mumbled thanks to my friend for taking me home, but I never properly thanked him for his charitable act of rescuing me from a scene that, in my oblivious state, had gone horribly wrong, and would have ended worse. I didn't know how to thank him. If I saw him at school or called to thank him and let him know how much I appreciated his kindness, I'd be opening myself up to possibly having to talk to somebody about these exasperating emotions I was going through. Or worse yet, I might have to admit that I wasn't strong enough to handle things on my own like I was sure I could. That would be admitting to a vulnerability I was not yet prepared to accept. Son of a bitch, this was hard.

The unsettling truth was I missed my dad more than I let on. To make matters worse, I was tormented by guilt and the perceived unfairness of never getting to say good-bye to him.

Why couldn't I have just stayed up until they got home that night? Was my piddly-ass cold that bad? Why didn't I wake up later on when they headed off to the hospital, with one never to return? Were they panicked? Scared? If I had been given the chance, what would I have said? What would he have said? If I had gotten to say good-bye, would the depth and breadth of my grief be any different?

I never said anything to my friend, and he never spoke of that night either. I think to some extent, it's a guy thing. No touchy, feely stuff allowed. Whatever. I resolved to be emotionally stronger, at least in public anyway. I guess the word is more "stoic." Man, I fortified those walls around me and built them even higher. You know, I just wanted to be freaking NORMAL. I just wanted to feel NORMAL, whatever the hell that was.

If it's not too late, thank you Jeff for your act of kindness on that summer night so very long ago.

Chapter 7

"But in the grey of the morning,
my mind becomes confused.
Between the dead and the sleeping,
and the road that I must choose.

I'm looking for someone to change my life,
I'm looking for a miracle in my life.
And if you could see
what it's done to me,
to lose the love I knew,
could safely lead me to
the land I once knew,
to learn as we grow old
the secrets of our soul."

From the song "Question"
By The Moody Blues

Sonnet XLIII

"How do I love thee? Let me count the ways.
I love thee to the depth and breadth and height
My soul can reach, when feeling out of sight
for the ends of Being and ideal Grace.
I love thee to the level of everyday's
most quiet need, by sun and candle-light.
I love thee freely, as men strive for Right;
I love thee purely, as they turn from Praise.
I love thee with the passion put to use
in my old griefs, and with my childhood's faith.
I love thee with a love I seemed to lose
with my lost saints, -I love thee with the breath,
smiles, tears, of all my life! – and, if God choose,
I shall but love thee better after death."

"Sonnets From The Portuguese"
By Elizabeth Barrett Browning

Diary Of A _____ Teenager

Selected entries from the year 1975

*(with present day commentary benefited by
36 years of hindsight)*

(OK, let's be honest about this. I didn't keep a diary back in
1975. Not then, not ever. But if I had, it would have come
pretty damn close to looking like this.)

January 1, 1975

The year 1974 was total shit. Good riddance. Put a fork in it,
as they say, and let's get the hell out of here. There's nowhere
to go but up, and I think maybe we're finally going to get back
to fairly normal routines in our lives.

(Not so fast young whippersnapper. Grief doesn't simply disappear with the turning of a calendar page. I wanted to believe we could simply wipe the slate clean with a new year and return to that "normal life" for which I kept pining. I soon discovered 1975 brought reruns of particularly difficult calendar dates we resigned ourselves to writing off as bad, sad days. There were the usual national and religious holidays to navigate through and around again, and there would be first anniversaries to contend with as well. Our happiness would be fleeting, and melancholy was unavoidable.)

February 5th

Today was dad's birthday. The first since his death, and the first of all his birthdays to come that would mark his eternal age of 42. Woke up early and we all attended early mass with mom. I spent the rest of the day basically keeping my head down and getting through it as best I could. I didn't talk about the significance of this day with any of my friends. They wouldn't understand, and if they had, why be a downer and make everyone feel uncomfortable. Not a whole lot of talk around the dinner table tonight.

March 24th

Today is my birthday. The first since my dad died, the first of all my birthdays to come that he will never see. I turned 17 years old today. Mom made my favorite dinner and an angel food cake for dessert. Sat through a ragged rendition of "Happy Birthday," and then went out with the guys. We bought beer and cigarettes and met up with a bunch of people at Sunnyside Park. Things got a little out of hand, and the cops showed up and broke up the party. Drove around for awhile drinking beer and blasting "Free Bird" from Mike's 8 track player.

March 30th

Today is Easter Sunday; the first since my dad died. We celebrated the Risen Christ by going to church. Christ has died. Christ is Risen. Christ will come again. Somewhere in those words there's a connection to dad, maybe even solace. Afterwards, mom made a great brunch and we spent the rest of the day stuffing ourselves with candy and hard-boiled eggs.

April 6th

Today is my sister's 16th birthday. The first since my dad died. Dad wasn't around to teach her to drive; so that was left for me to do. I think she'll pass her driver's test, but she scared the hell out of me on more than one occasion while out on the road with her. Most of the time I made her drive around the roads of the cemetery, it seemed like a safe enough place to be.

April 16th

Today is mom's birthday. The first since …… What would dad have done for mom today? Something better than the stupid card I got her, or the dinner we tried to fix her, or our singing that sucked.

May 5th

Today is the first anniversary of dad's death. Some people say "passing". Why sugar-coat it? He died. I don't know what to think about this day. I don't know what to say or how I should feel. Well, I know I feel like shit. And I know there really isn't anything to say, because if I do say something, the tears will fall. We woke up early and attended mass with mom. Afterwards, mom took us out to breakfast. The waffles were good. I guess it's better to feel like crap on a full stomach than on an empty one. I spent the rest of the day doing what I do best;

keeping my head down, intent on getting through it without revealing the significance of the day to the outside world. I'm laying here in bed, in the dark, listening to Elton sing "Funeral For A Friend" and I can't stop thinking how much I miss dad, how much I miss the way things were, how freaking hard this is. Dad had a birthday, now he has a deathday as well. I can't stop these frigging tears.

(Hmmm…. All these years later, and I still don't quite know what to think about this date. Dad's birthday is ok. That day comes, and it's like, hey, today is dad's birthday. He would have been…. years old today. If there is some sadness with that day, it's in the realization of just how much he has missed out on over the years. Deathdays are another matter. In general, these days are only remembered by an intimate group of acquaintances. There are exceptions of course. There's a whole generation that knows the date John Kennedy was shot, and September 11th has been seared into all our brains. As for dad's deathday, I'm a member of a select group that remembers May 5th, 1974. I'm haunted by that date. I've learned to live with that date.)

June 15th

Today is Father's Day. Round 2. The second Father's Day without dad came and went; we were learning how to maneuver around the landscape of this particular holiday. In our home, there was a certain quietness that surrounded days like today, days like anniversaries and holidays. We all missed dad. We all sensed the pain that dwelled within each other's heart. But to talk about those thoughts and feelings we shared, well, that risked opening a floodgate of tears that would make us feel all the more miserable than we already are. It was too much to risk, better to keep my mouth shut; it's the best way I know to get through days like today.

June 22nd

Today was mom and dad's wedding anniversary. We woke up and went to early mass with mom. This day absolutely sucks. Of all the days of the year we have to suffer through, this day cuts the deepest. Mom's anguish left me feeling like a help-less bag of shit. I tried to say something, I tried to offer some words of consolation and sympathy without making mom and me cry. But I failed miserably; I was no match for the loss mom was feeling. The quiet in our house is awful.

(There was, and still is to this day, a picture of mom and dad on mom's bedroom dresser. It was not a formal, posed picture, but rather a photo of a spontaneous, representative moment in time of an everyday man and woman with arms around each other, and big smiles of contentment on their faces. Their eyes, looking out at you, conveyed a joyful message of singular com-panionship. The essence of that photo had been ripped away from my mother. In mom's eyes, and in her heart, the love they shared could never be replaced. She refused to refer to their love in the past tense. She was determined to carry their love in her heart for the rest of her life. Death could remove the physical presence of my father, but by God, she would conquer Death by keeping their love alive.)

July 4th

It's the Fourth of July! In past years, this day was a very big deal in our neighborhood. Fireworks, picnic, the whole bit. Our next door neighbors were really into the fireworks, and every year they were in charge of the fireworks show put on in the field across the street from our houses. Like today, it was always hotter than hell, but that didn't stop us from spending the day lighting "black cats", smoke bombs, and "snakes". As we got older, we graduated to bottle rocket fights and sneaking beer from the coolers our parents packed for the picnics. But this year, there was a certain awkwardness about the picnic. The neighbor's small talk seemed a little too happy-to-see-me for my liking. I wanted to be somewhere else. I grabbed a plate of food, and made my escape as soon as I could. I drank beer alone in the air conditioned quiet of our home. I don't think anyone missed me.

(36 years later, I look at these dates, and these first 6 months of the year must have felt like I was running some kind of gauntlet of misery. It seemed like an unending saga of melancholy. I struggled mightily to get to that place of normalcy I talked about. Then those dates would loom on the horizon and suddenly arrive, and those emotional wounds of mine, which were just starting to scab over, would get picked open again. I'm going to stop here with the diary thing. The entries would have gotten fewer and fewer anyway. You can refer back to Chapter 3 of this book, "Holiday Hell," to get the gist of the remaining holidays of 1975.)

I think you've got the general idea of what the year 1975 was like. It wasn't all bad, but grief tends to obscure the happier times. To put it bluntly, my faux diary does a pretty good job of documenting one long pity party. But impersonal, unfeeling time marched on. Of course it never slowed to wait for us to get our shit together as another year of dark anniversaries came and went, and then another year's, and another, and another. Although, it's true, over time those dreaded, hurtful dates softened into tolerable reminders of a father and a time that traveled farther and farther away from us. This is my third and final verse of the "time heals all wounds" crap. I found wounds do heal eventually, the scabs do fall off, if only because we, the survivors, are just as forgotten by the world as our own waning memories. At least, on the surface, things appear to be all right. And the scars that are left? Well, I guess they are as unsightly as you choose to allow them to be.

For me, there were these haunting questions that still came unannounced, unbidden by date or event. They were like an unwelcome visitor you have no desire to meet who keeps showing up, pounding on your door, and demanding, "Why didn't you take better care of yourself? Didn't you know what was at stake? How the hell could you leave us like this? And for the love of God, how could you cause so much pain for mom?" I knew these questions were unfair, and yet, for the longest time, every time they paid me a visit, I thought I was owed, deserved, answers.

Eventually, I was left with the frustrating realization that these shoot-from-the-hip, unanswerable questions weren't even relevant anymore. So, what the hell was? If I was going to somehow make my peace, I had to dig deeper for the more important questions. It was almost like the game show "Jeopardy," where the truthfulness of your answers is revealed by how you posed the questions. Pissed-off at the world and isolated by my own doing, I walked around as if I had on a set of blinders. Then for some inexplicable reason, one day the fog clears, a light bulb comes on, and it's as simple as walking by your mom's bedroom doorway. You peek in, and there on mom's dresser is that picture of eternal love, a truer picture there never was, speaking volumes to you. Sometimes what you are searching for is right in front of you the whole damn time. As I struggled to make sense of things, to ask the "right" questions, I thought, God, I want what they had.

Chapter 7 Heading: Diary Of A _____ Teenager

Interactive Reading!

You pick the word from the list below and fill in the blank!

Or, use your own word and become a co-author!

Awkward	Belligerent	Delinquent
Disrespectful	Drunk	Earnest
Fatherless	Foul-Mouthed	Grounded
Hungry	Idealistic	Lying
Mad	Miserable	Mumbling
Opinionated	Pimply	Pissed-Off
Pitiful	Pouting	Sad
Self-Centered	Sensitive	Sex-Crazed
Sleep-deprived	Smart-Ass	Sorry
Troubled	Unapproachable	Uncertain
Uncommunicative	Unhappy	Willful
	Wounded	

Chapter 8

"He who learns must suffer.
And even in our sleep
pain that cannot forget falls drop by drop upon the heart,
and in our own despair, against our will,
comes wisdom to us by the awful grace of God."

Aeschylus

"I went out walkin'
Through streets paved with gold....
...I passed by a thousand signs
Lookin' for my own name

I went out searchin'
Lookin' for one good man
A spirit who would not bend or break
Who would sit at his father's right hand
I went out walkin' with a Bible and a gun
The word of God lay heavy on my heart
I was sure I was the one

Yeah I went with nothin'
Nothin' but the thought of you
I went wandering"

From the song "The Wanderer"
Sung by Johnny Cash
Written by Larry Mullen, Paul Hewson,
Dave Evans, Adam Clayton

Death-Defying Acts of Stupidity …. and What The Hell Could It All Could Possibly Mean?

Cautionary note # 2 for all you young adults out there: The legalized age for any and all acts of stupidity has yet to be determined. The following story is a testament to this fact.

On a pleasant, clear spring night I went skiing to cap off the day-long celebration of my 18th birthday. Eighteenth birthdays were a big deal back in the day. They carried the same significance 21st birthdays do today. Turning 18 meant you were legally of age to drink adult beverages. Provided it had not been confiscated along the way, you could kiss that fake I.D. in your wallet good-bye! Now, this particular form of skiing did not involve water or snow. It did involve the use of a car's roof. Any kind of car really will do. In this particular story, the car was my friend's black 1970 Chevy Camaro. I was going "roof skiing," an early form of extreme sports yet to be seen on ESPN.

I climbed on top of my friend's car and lay in a prone position with my hands grasping each side of the car's roof edge. There was no luggage rack of course; that would be against the rules of idiocy. So with me spread-eagled on the roof, my friend headed out onto the suburban streets of Kansas City. Tentative at first- who in their right mind wouldn't be- my friend gradually overcame his fear of killing me and gleefully put the pedal to the metal. Wind and lights rushed by. I felt as if I was in one of those time-lapse photos of city traffic with the colored tracers preceding the cars. My senses were incredibly heightened, and my pulse was racing. There was an exhilaration that screamed forth, "I am invincible!" What could be better than this? Why, I bet if we went on the highway, hell's bells, that would be the ultimate rush! Off we went to find the nearest entrance ramp, and soon my friend was accelerating onto east bound 435 highway.

It was at this point it began to occur to me that what I was doing was incredibly stupid, not to mention, insanely dangerous. I was now hanging on to dear life as we hurdled down the highway of an 80-mile-an-hour wind tunnel. My senses were still heightened alright, but my exhilaration had been replaced by sheer terror. Exiting off the highway after what seemed like forever, but really only minutes, the car came mercifully to a stop. I shakily slid off the roof, grateful to be standing on solid ground. Relief flooded over me as I got into the car, and, damn! Would I have a story to tell for the rest of my life! I had cheated sure death and lived to tell about it. These delusional thoughts of grandeur were quickly followed by another more sobering thought: My God, what the hell was I thinking? I sure as hell didn't hear "My turn!" coming out of my friend's mouth.

Cautionary note # 3 to all you out there reading this: Telling my little roof-skiing story was the easy part of this chapter; now comes the hard part. Somehow I've got to decipher, interpret, and convey to you in a way that makes perfect sense what was going through my mind at that time in my life. An iffy proposition at best by my calculations, an impossible task you might conclude, especially if you happened to be acquainted with me back then. If philosophical discussion or psychological analysis bores you, I'd recommend you skip the rest of this chapter and move right on to the next one. Should you opt to continue reading and this ends up to be a convoluted mess, I'm sorry, but I warned you. If somehow I pull this off, well, I guess I won't know whether to be happy I explained myself well enough for you to understand, or sad you know exactly what I'm talking about.

Since that birthday night long ago, I've rarely told this epic, thrill-riding story. It's not because of any misplaced humility on my part, but because it didn't take long for me to realize this was something I could never be proud of, what with demonstrating my stupidity and all. There were other dumb-as-rocks activities I could bore you with, but let's just say there were things I did to convince myself I was in control of my own destiny, not God's evil twin, Death. In Pop Psych 101 parlance, I was subconsciously seeking the connectivity between my father's death, a Higher Being and my own life. Or to put it another way, what I just said is just a bunch of bullshit, and subconsciously or not, I was just being an idiot. Of course the reality was all of the above, to one extent or another depending on the circumstances at the time of my various misadventures.

Perhaps because of this cradle Catholic's faithful naiveté, I never thought of my struggles following dad's death as a me vs God issue. I was more hurt than angry at God. I felt like the little kid who's been left out of the playground game. It's like I was thinking what the hell just happened here? My feelings are hurt, and it's just not fair. Call it grief if you want, but it just plain sucks. Who's to blame for this? Dad? God? Death? Because there's got to be someone or something to blame. Yeah, Death seemed like a prime suspect. I just needed to somehow transform it into an entity unto itself like The Grim Reaper or the spirit in "A Christmas Carol" that scares the hell out of Ebenezer Scrooge.

What about God? I was brought up to believe God is good. I had first-hand experience death was bad. Was it as simple as that? Or could God and Death be both good and bad? God seemed to operate on a whole different level this mere mortal of 18 was having trouble understanding. I chose to take a measure of comfort in the belief that God had somehow given me a heads-up about the loss of my father through those dreams I had experienced growing up. Therefore, I was willing to give God an uncomprehending benefit of the doubt. And Dad? I knew deep down he had been given no choice in the matter. I was willing to hold out hope that dad had not totally abandoned us and that he could somehow be a guardian angel for my family and me.

Without looking for or wanting to, I saw the tentacles of Death everywhere in my world. And it seemed to me I was getting more than my fair share of the Reaper's reality and the consequences that followed. That's just life, you might say. It's a proven fact, everyone is going to die. But at my malleable age, every death that touched my life looked like a conspiracy of some sort that pushed the limits of my understanding of ....what? All this crap we're talking about here. Was I being picked on? Of course not, but I still took it personally, and frankly, I was getting a little pissed-off about it.

Everyone is going to die. In the spring of my senior year, our principal died. He was the kind of person who took the time to learn every student's name. He was kind and genuinely interested in me. As a Jesuit priest, he lived the Jesuit creed "a man for others" to the fullest. There was no doubt about it; he was one of the good ones. He was about my father's age too, and dammit, too young to die. A staff member on our school newspaper asked me to write something about him for the upcoming issue, which I gladly agreed to do. I guess he thought since I had experience with this sort of thing, not the writing part, the premature death thing, I would be a good choice. I said all the right things in that article, and what I wrote was heartfelt. Yet, our principal's death surely seemed to reinforce my unpublished working hypothesis that his death was yet another example of the Reaper's work. If there was going to be a bad guy in this story, someone or something that I could wrap my grieving mind around and gain some measure of pain relief, he or it was going to be named "Death," aka "The Reaper."

It was damn complicated, this whole understanding of death and its sidekick grief. Deep down I knew there was more to death than turning it into some sort of action figure, and I knew grief went deeper than simply assigning blame. Not to make excuses here, but when you are a man-child going through your days in an adolescent fog of self-absorption, it's pretty difficult to sort things out in any kind of way that makes sense. If mankind's greatest minds were still trying to figure it out, what chance in hell did I have? I made death into something tangible I could relate to. It was my way of grieving, whether it was healthy or not. Death became my mortal enemy simply because of what it had done to my family and me.

Let's throw one more ingredient into the recipe I concocted for my understanding and treatment of Death. Let's call it the fear factor. I vowed to be fearless in the face of Death. That was the easiest thing to do in my young life. The potential for my own death did not scare me. In fact, my sometimes moronic behavior, the roof-skiing incident being Exhibit A, demonstrated a willingness to dare Death to scare me. It was like, "Come on m---f---, give me your best shot." However, my fearlessness began to waiver when the issue became not the theoretical death I taunted, but the imagined or real death of others. Fear became palpable when the hypothesis became what if so and so died? What would that do to me? Then there would also be those very real times, like the death of our school principal, when Death visited my life and robbed me once again of a friend or loved one. Oh, how my bravado in the face of death melted away as once again I was reminded of my powerlessness.

Consequently, to this day I have never been able to successfully beat back those, oh let's say irrational-leaning, fears that creep into my consciousness when a loved one becomes sick, or leaves me to take an extended trip, or hell, just a trip to the grocery store. As soon as that person walks out the door, any manner of deadly scenarios could go through my imagination; kidnappings, murders, car crashes, you name it. There might be slow, agonizing cancerous deaths or the suddenly violent, unsuspecting kind of deaths. Let your imagination run wild! I could, and still can, scare the hell out of myself.

Because of these, ok I admit it, irrational fears, if there were issues to be resolved or hurt feelings to mend, I always felt it better to make amends with that person before a trip started or before the day ended. Just now, rather than later. Not because of any altruistic reason on my part, but because you never know, Death could take that person away from me at any moment. And shit, wouldn't that be bad to be left with the lasting memory of the argument you had with that person just before they died? Or I'll end up praying to and bargaining with God, " Please don't take this person from me. If you have to take someone, let it be me. Please Lord, for my sake; keep them healthy and safe. Besides, You already did this to me once, remember? Surely You wouldn't do it to me again, would You? And…." Wait just a minute, am I confusing God and Death now? Are they one in the same? Years later, and I'm still trying to wrap my freaking pea brain around this.

I'm back on top of that car, and it might as well be my life we're talking about here, because when it comes to death, I'm not in control. I'm on God's time. It's that time continuum we've all experienced when minutes seem to last forever. A lifetime is a minute in God's time. Who am I to think I have

any say in the matter of death? Death is not God's evil twin.
Death is not a Being. Death is an instrument of God, and there
is not a damn thing you or I can do about its inevitability. I'm
sick to death of talking about all this, and I'm sure you're sick
to death of reading about it (I warned you). Before I lose it and
call it all bullshit, here's the last thing I'm going to say on the
subject: death is His way of saying you're on My time, and
time's up. Deal with it.

Chapter 9

"I have not seen him in two years,
but Time does not deserve my tears…

In the quiet of night I pray to him;
asking to be always at my side,
asking for guidance and comfort again,
asking to be like the man in whom I confide."

The best excerpts from a pretty bad poem entitled "T.E.B."

By TJB, a well-meaning young man struggling to put pen to
paper the emotions of a wounded heart, circa 1976.

"I don't know where I can turn…
Won't You show me where to go?

Give me a revelation
Show me what to do
'Cause I've been trying to find my way
I haven't got a clue."

From the song "Revelation"
By Third Day

Christmas Ghosts

Growing up, Christmas time at our home was divided into religious and secular celebrations. On Christmas Eve, Santa Claus paid us a visit. When we were younger, dad would herd the family into the station wagon Christmas Eve, and we'd go out looking at people's Griswaldesque holiday light decorations. Sometime later we would arrive back home to find that Santa had magically come and gone, considerately leaving presents neatly stacked by name on the family room floor. Then all joyous hell broke loose. Wrapping paper flew, Christmas music played and the camera flashed and temporarily blinded you. Presents opened, and basking in the after-glow of our Yuletide haul, we retired to the kitchen to feast on freshly baked Christmas cookies and perhaps brave a cup of eggnog.

We thought it was pretty cool Santa made our house one of his first stops every year. Speaking now as a parent, I know mom and dad were hip to not having to get up at the crack of dawn to watch us open presents. Then on Christmas Day, we celebrated the holy birth of Jesus. The day began by attending morning mass and ended with a wonderful meal lovingly prepared by mom. Christmas Dinner always included the obligatory photo-op of all of us, spit and polished, sitting at the dining room table. For a grand finale, mom served a dessert of angel food birthday cake in honor of baby Jesus.

When I was 14, I received a cassette tape player and recorder for Christmas. Back in the day, home-audio recording was still something of a novelty, at least in my neck of the woods. So it was a pretty big deal when I got one of those cassette players. I immediately started recording the audio highlights of that Christmas Eve. Amongst the raucous sounds of wrapping paper being torn open and our happy exclamations was the sound of my father's voice happily answering our shouts of "look what I got!" Somehow that recording survived my youthful enthusiasm for taping the latest top 40 songs played on the radio at the time. Years later it has become this rare and wonderful artifact, a time machine that can carry me back in time through the living sound of his voice.

The second event I recorded that Christmas season was the Chiefs' playoff game against the Miami Dolphins on Christmas Day. Many football fans remember the game as the longest play-off game in NFL history and one of the all-time greatest games ever played. At the time, home games were not broadcast on TV like they are today, so I faithfully listened to the game on the radio. I taped the announcer's play-by-play description of the action, and depending on the Chiefs' fortunes, added my own, sometimes ecstatic, other times disappointed, commentary as well. It was goof-ball stuff by a 14-year-old kid, but this tape has also survived all these years. The earnestness of my commentating makes it embarrassingly funny to listen to, but there is also something poignant about hearing that boy document a historic football game in his own heartfelt words. Come to think of it, I experience the same kind of feelings when I hear the recording of dad's voice. It's kind of hard to describe what those feelings are exactly, but they're like the emotions evoked by great music or the saddest song you've ever heard.

For me, this particular holy day became as memorable as the game itself because of how the game affected mom's Christmas dinner. The game was tied at the end of regulation, and continued into sudden-death overtime. As the game wore on and on, the time for mom's dinner was pushed back further and further. Of course the longer the game went, the harder it was for mom to preserve her carefully prepared dinner in perfect serving condition. Finally, and tragically for this young fan, the game ended in defeat for our Chiefs. In mom's eyes, dinner was just as tragically ruined, and her usual sunny disposition had withered away with it. It was one of the few times I ever saw my mom truly angry. Dinner was not particularly festive for those of us who had lived and died with the Chiefs in their epic battle or for those of us whose dinner had been ruined by a blasphemous, stupid football game. "Joy To The World" was the farthest thing from our minds as we glumly sat at the dinning room table. In fact, I don't think we even bothered with the obligatory holiday picture that year.

Fast forward to 1976. By my 18th year, the audio and visual memories of my father were fading away at an alarming rate. It was upsetting that I had trouble recalling what he looked and sounded like. I felt it was almost like cheating if I had to look at old pictures of him to refresh my memory, but that was what it was coming down to. The picture I treasured most was a photo taken of dad and me on my 16th birthday. We are standing in front of the family room fireplace, our family's traditional picture taking place. I am dressed in '70s chic, wearing plaid bell-bottom pants and a dark-blue sweater vest. My hair is daringly longer than the military-style crewcut I had worn since first grade. Dad is doing his level best to keep up with the times by wearing slacks with a white belt (with matching white shoes), a plaid shirt and a light blue sweater vest. Two years after that picture was taken, I would enviously stare at the boy who had a father to stand next to. Admittedly, I tended to look upon the picture's subject matter with rose-colored glasses. It would have almost been sacrilegious for me to view it any other way.

Today, I look at that picture and see staring back at me a boy who idolized his father. I see a man-child who felt such happiness when he could make his dad laugh or please him in some way. With the benefit of years gone by, I look at that picture and recall what you couldn't see: the winds of adolescent discontent that had begun to blow, and the troubled waters our relationship was just beginning to navigate. Musical tastes, hair length, clothing styles, life styles, political thought and people we admired were all becoming subjects of debate between us. Yes, I liked nothing more than to please my dad, but I was becoming uncomfortably aware he was definitely old school.

Talk about a clash of cultures. Dad rocked to guys like Burt Bacharach and Ed Ames. I rocked to, well, pretty much anything that was rock-n-roll. Dad actually had an album entitled "Ballads of the Green Berets." Even today, I still shake my head at that one. Dad was not particularly receptive to long-haired hippy types and Vietnam peace demonstrations. I kinda saw their point. I admired Martin Luther King and Bobby Kennedy. Dad was decidedly circumspect about expressing his opinions about them and the causes they championed. I was mortified to find out dad had voted for Barry Goldwater in the '64 presidential election. Dad was a city kid who boxed in his youth and later worked at the corner butcher's shop in his hometown of Cleveland. He encouraged an eye-for-an-eye approach to problem-solving when he felt my response to disagreements with other kids was a little too much like turn-the-other-cheek. I could go on, but I think you get the picture.

On closer inspection of that picture, maybe you could deduce some of what might have been had he lived by noticing how we stood next to each other. Side by side, yes, but dad with his hands down at his side, and me with my left hand, adorned with a wide leather-banded wrist watch, clasping the wrist of my right arm in front of me, both of us staring straight ahead at the camera with half-smiles plastered on our faces. Not exactly a warm and huggable Kodak moment. If you put it all together when considering the big picture, our body language, my 20/20 hindsight insider information and 36 years later, there was no doubt about it, we were finding less and less common ground to stand on. The young gun was beginning to chafe under the old man's ways.

At age 18 there might have been rose-colored glasses involved, but I looked at that picture with a maturity earned the hard way. I saw the reality of a man who would forever look the same, who would never age, never change, never know what it would be like to live in my world right here, right now. No matter what my age, I would see a man who would never be a father to his children as they got older or a grandfather to his children's children. I saw a husband who would never grow old with his wife. How I've wondered over the years how different my life would have been if he could have stuck around. Wondered how he and I would have gotten along and how my life choices would have changed. I'm not the same person I was in that picture. Dad will always be the same.

At those sorriest of times when wondering about what might have been spiraled into melancholy self-pity, I'd dig out the old Christmas audio cassette from my 14th year. I would jump in the car with my trusty cassette player and just take-off driving, nowhere in particular, and reboot my memory's audio transmission of the sound of my father's voice. And damn if I didn't hear myself asking the same tormenting questions every time I played that tape: "Are you there? Are you with me? Can you hear these unspoken thoughts of mine?" Over and over again I would listen to the tape as I drove the streets and hear the happy, innocent sounds of a family unblemished by heartbreaking loss. Over and over again I would listen for any kind of answer to my questions. I'd hear the shouts of "look what I got!" and plead, "give me a sign." Then I'd hear the fearless voice of an innocent boy engrossed in a game that ended in sudden-death. I cried every time.

Chapter 10

"Goodbye to Teacher's true love so soon,
tiger lily memories forever bloom.
God, your strength, rock, true light,
a Faith burning bright in our life."

From a half-way decent poem entitled "Carole"
By TJB, a well-meaning, loving son

"There is a season and a time
for every purpose under heaven."

From the song "Turn! Turn! Turn!"
By Pete Seeger, adapted from Ecclesiastes

The Surviving Parent

I never saw or heard my parents argue. I never heard them use foul language or raise their voices to each other. I never felt, as children often do, the tension of an unhappy marriage. What I did see was a truly wonderful example of love. After almost 17 years of marriage, my parents still addressed each other by their terms of endearment: "Honey" and "Elwood." The happiness they shared enabled us kids to enjoy a happy childhood. Then one day in May, Honey forever lost her El-wood. From that moment on, whatever Fate decreed she would face on her own.

While it was not a strategy specifically discussed and agreed upon between us, my siblings and I rarely mentioned dad in mom's presence after he died. Nor was the question of how the hell this could happen to our family ever thrown out there for one and all to hear and expound upon. It was best to keep that sort of question to ourselves, to be figured out as best we could by ourselves. There was to be no biblical wailing and gnashing of teeth in our house, no rants about the unfairness of it all. Why make our mother more miserable than she already was?

Any activity or conversation that posed a threat of adding to mom's sadness was to be avoided at all cost. As far as I was concerned, I didn't care what the hell my brother and sisters did, just be damn sure you didn't get caught and make things worse on mom. I thought we were helping mom by locking away our memories of dad and steeling ourselves against the various and sundry emotions of loss we were all going through. No crying was a good thing. Not talking about dad or anything really that made us sad, which then made mom sad, was a good thing. Except as a result of our efforts to protect mom, and perhaps ourselves too, mom was left with no one, no one, to share her grief with.

Mom had always been the comforter, sympathizer and fixer of all that was broken in our world. Now we found ourselves attempting to fill that role. We weren't very good at it. She had her good days and bad days as she waged her battle to overcome her grief. It was unsettling to see mom struggle so. We were quick to recognize those days when mom was there but not really, as she performed almost by rote her motherly duties. She fixed our meals, cleaned the house, even asked how our day was. But we saw that her mind was elsewhere. It seemed best to leave her alone on those days, to bother her as little as possible with our own issues of the day.

There were times though, when I let my guard down. Most of the time it would be when it was just mom and me sitting at the kitchen table. It would often be in the evening when the house was quiet after my siblings had scattered to their rooms after dinner. The only light left in the kitchen coming from the fixture above our table. The rest was shadows and silence, creating the perfect mood for reflection and confession. Mom had a great knack for catching me in those times when I was in the mood for feeling sorry for myself and vulnerable to discussions that would turn my inward view outward.

The subject matter always started with me, and it could go

anywhere after that. But the conversation never turned to her problems. No matter how hard I tried to keep it from happening, inevitably my self-pity would seep out during the course of these heart-felt conversations, and mom would inevitably talk about how dad must be so very proud of me. If I was in a particularly dark mood, those words rang hollow to me. I would be angry with myself for bringing up whatever we were talking about in the first place. Mostly though, I took them as small consolation, but still nice to hear on occasions such as these. That was a comfort I had to live with.

In the fall of my senior year, a year and a half after my father's death, mom asked if we could sit down and talk. The alarm bells started to go off, but I was pretty sure I wasn't in trouble. I did a pretty good job of covering my tracks when my behavior outside the home was somewhat questionable. I wasn't in a particularly reflective mood either, and didn't have anything weighing on my mind at the time, but I could see she did. It didn't take long for mom to get to the point: Would I be interested in attending the University of Indiana? She was thinking about moving our family back to Fort Wayne where she still had family. The university wouldn't be too far away. IU was a good school, and we could visit the campus to check it out if I'd like to. It sure would be nice to be closer to her family. What did I think? Even as dense as I could be at times, I could hear the hope in that question.

What did I think? What did I think. Caught off guard, it took me a minute to regroup and pronounce my sentence. There were all kinds of reasons why this was an absolutely terrible idea; it would be a nightmare. I had my heart set on attending KU. My friends and girlfriend were here. Everyone and everything I was sure of was here in this world I had so carefully created for myself. I couldn't imagine leaving my cocoon world, not now. Mom would be asking way too much of me and my siblings. Surely my brother and sisters would feel the same way. No way, no how would I want to move to Indiana.

We sat at the kitchen table in the lengthening quiet of the house. Where the hell was everyone? The only sound was the "tick-tock, tick-tock," of our grandfather clock counting down the demise of any thoughts, of any hopes, my mom had about moving back home. I was sealing mom's fate. My selfishness was heard loud and clear. There would be no help coming, no comfort taken from leaning on family close by. It would be just her, the surviving parental spouse. With her quiet, unselfish "ok," the conversation ended. I, for my part, breathed a huge sigh of relief, and conveniently ignored the pangs of guilt I felt for what I had just done. I left mom sitting there at the table, alone in the shadows, as I quickly beat a path back to the sanctuary of my room. The topic of moving was never mentioned again.

In her darkest moments, mom must have questioned God's "plan" for her life. Talk about a test of faith; was this how a good and just God treated one created in His own image? She had every right to demand the meaning of it all, to ask where the good was in her sudden, inexplicable loss. But I'm just as sure that whatever anger mom felt succumbed to her indomitable belief that there is "a time for every purpose under the heavens," to quote the book of Ecclesiastes. Mom prayed and prayed for the understanding of that purpose under heaven. She knew that's where her healing would begin and where her comfort would come from.

The physical evidence of dad's existence began to disappear from our home. My father's pipes and tobacco that sat on the family room end table were quietly put away. As were his coats that hung in the entry closet and the book he had been reading at the time. The top of the dresser in my parent's bedroom that tended to collect dad's knick-knacks and pocket change was cleaned off. Their bathroom left with only 1 toothbrush on the sink. Their room became mom's room.

Mom was slowly letting go. Not of her love for dad, but the life she had known for the past 17 years. Left alone as the surviving parent, to her great credit she saw there really was no other choice in the matter but to soldier on alone. I believe, I know, her prayers were answered. Talk about the power of prayer. Thank God mom's tremendous faith in Him and great love of dad gave her the strength to fight her terrible loneliness and accept her daunting task. There came a day when I surreptitiously walked into mom's bedroom and opened her closet door. On what used to be dad's side of the closet I saw nothing but open space.

One of my favorite books is John Irving's "A Prayer For Owen Meany." In that book, the title character is not what you would call "normal." Many people considered him to be deformed or damaged goods. At the story's climax, Owen performs an act of heroism that we ultimately see he had prepared his whole life for. In my story, it's certainly not out of the ordinary for a child to lose a parent or to have their father die on them. But in our insular, suburban America, it's not all that common-place either. There was an awareness on my part of becoming somehow different. Maybe I even felt as if I were being looked upon, in an unwanted sympathetic sort of way, as damaged goods.

So I thought God must have something awfully special planned for me to have put me through such misery. It was my fate. No longer ordinary, I decided I must have been chosen by Him for something extraordinary, for some kind of heroic deed. I was Owen, if you will, singled out for greatness, not simply for being a fatherless son. Never mind the fact that in Irving's story Owen's act of heroism was born out of complete unselfishness, while my destined heroism was tainted by the selfishness of self-absorption. I guess I felt I was somehow owed a hero's success or acclaim for the dues I had been forced to pay. All I sought was a balancing of the books if you will. That was only fair, wasn't it?

For many years, my story book imaginings of being anointed by God as a hero-in-waiting grudgingly stayed with me. Slowly those imaginings gave way to a realization that there is no quid pro quo in life. It's a hard lesson to learn. Fate generally does not have a way of evening things out. Sure, we all know that person who lives the charmed life, where everything comes so easily and abundantly. But for the rest of us, life, more often than not, is dealing with challenges and adversity. That's where the underappreciated kind of heroism comes into play. Heroism can be the dramatic headline news version, or it can simply be the exemplary way a person faces the ordinary and sometimes extraordinary challenges that are placed before them. That person is the kind of hero who lives their life unconditionally and unselfishly, performing with an unassuming grace and equanimity while facing life's daily trials. Like the woman who sat across from you in the lengthening quiet of your home's kitchen, her hands prayerfully clasped on her lap, sacrificing herself with the utterance of a simple "ok."

Chapter 11

"It's the thing hammered into the father all his life,
and thundering now in these late-summer skies over
Yankee Stadium.

The glory of hope at the death of expectation."

From a Sports Illustrated article
By Gary Smith

"Occurred to me the other day
You've been gone now a couple years
Well, I guess it takes awhile
For someone to really disappear
And I remember where I was
When the word came about you
It was a day much like today
The sky was bright, and wide, and blue

And I wonder where you are
And if the pain ends when you die
And I wonder if there was
Some better way to say goodbye"

From the song "Goodbye"
By Patty Griffin

A Retreat With Gridiron Glory

In a scene that would have fit nicely in a movie like "Dead Poet's Society," the weather was frosty cold. Grey skies hung low, burdened with the potential for snow. On a barren field, the pick-up football game participants ran in a biting wind that kicked up the dried brown leaves of an autumn fading fast into memory. Breath clouds floated in the air, shrouding the shaggy-haired youths who paid little heed to the cold. They were rather more intent on smashing the guy with the ball. Happy to be outside, no matter what the weather, the boys were releasing pent-up energy after a day spent cooped-up indoors contemplating the mysteries of life, God and themselves.

During our senior year, we were required to participate in a two-day spiritual retreat at a seminary just outside Kansas City. The retreats were intended to be for groups of 50 or so boys at a time. Attendees were then divided into smaller discussion groups upon their arrival. One minute you're sharing heart-felt thoughts with the guy next to you about what it means to be a Christian and the next minute you're knocking the crap out of him on the football field. That's life at an all-boys Jesuit high school. Faculty led the small groups in prayer services and talks on topics ranging from the abiding presence, or lack there of, of God in our lives to how we are or should be leading our lives. Quiet time in our dorm room was also set aside each day for individual reflection on what we were somehow miraculously doing right and evidently screwing up.

As a rule of thumb, what you got out of these retreats was in direct proportion to the amount of effort you put into them. By the age of 18, most of us were mature enough to give a what-the-hell commitment to a spiritual exercise billed as helping us get in touch with our inner-self. As an additional bonus it got you out of school for a couple of days. Be that as it may, one could only take so much serious reflection before the attention-deficit kicked in and the need to get in touch with our physical side and play some no-holds-barred tackle football came out. Pads and helmet not required.

For any boy growing up who loves sports, you dream about being the star player or the guy who wins the game for your team on the last play of the game. On that particular November day on an anonymous field, in a game with utterly no significance to the outside world, I was the star. It was the best football game I ever played in, and the self-satisfaction I carried away from that game has stayed with me for a lifetime. We divided into teams and played with a reckless abandon. We were unconstrained by our every day adolescent worries, by people's perceptions of us or our own perceptions of ourselves. When I got the ball, it would take two and three guys to tackle me. I would not go down. I chased down ball carriers on the other team and smashed into them with an enthusiasm that guaranteed they were going no farther. I don't think the organizers of our retreat intended this recreational break to be the memorable event of our retreat, but it was for me. It was further proof the Spirit does move in mysterious ways.

One of our last retreat activities was to write a letter to ourselves describing what was going on in our lives. We wrote about things we were ok sharing in our discussion groups and private things we could never talk about, but weighed on our minds nevertheless. This touchy-feely exercise was a little weird to me. Why bother writing down what I already knew in my head for me to read later? Despite my reservations, I decided to play along and give it a try. I generally liked to play my cards close to the vest, so if I was going to commit my most personal thoughts to paper, I wanted to be sure I got it right, I didn't want to look stupid here. After a long time of staring at the blank paper taunting me on my desk, I finally got the words down I wanted to say. The letters were sealed and collected by our moderators, and they were then sent to our homes a month later as a reminder that our retreat had either been total bullshit or an opportunity for new discoveries about ourselves.

I still have that letter, and it's nice to see I chose the latter course of action. It's an earnest account of a young man at a time in his life when he was struggling to see the world through the eyes of a functioning adult, but often acting as a naive self-aware boy. Much of life's angst for a boy crossing over to manhood is there in his penciled words. The concerns he had about college, his special feelings for a certain girl, that self-esteem-building football performance, God and how He fits into all of this, and of course, living without a father.

Thoughts of my dad were never far from my mind, and they were there during that retreat long ago. During our group discussions it dawned on me my classmates no longer saw me as the unfortunate kid whose father died when we were sophomores. It was slowly sinking into my thick head that their perceptions of me, or anyone's for that matter, were indeed formed to a certain extent by the cards dealt me. But more significantly, they were formed by the words I spoke and the actions I took. In other words, I defined who I was or who I was going to be by how I conducted my life. The clarity of people's perceptions was dictated by how I responded to both fortune and adversity. I would have the final say on the matter.

There was no denying that the death of my dad forever altered the landscape of my life, but that tragedy didn't have to end up defining it. During this time, I first glimpsed the great gift my father left me. The first fruits of discovery are there in the letter I wrote myself. I was beginning to understand that through his death, my father had given me the wonderful gift of freedom to be whoever I wanted to be and choose however I wanted to live my life. My God, there it was! I was free to be me. There would be no excuses to give or blame to assign. My horizons limited only by my own narrowness of mind. It was like freaking Christopher Columbus discovering the world wasn't flat.

This growing sense of self-determination charged my football play that day with a tremendous feeling of joy and freedom. I had broken the mold. I was outside the perception box. I was almost unrecognizable to my classmates on the field who had known me since freshman year. When the game ended, wouldn't you know, my team was on the losing end of the score. Why was it that two of my most important sports- imitating -life moments ended in defeat? Remember my "Rocky" imitation on the wrestling mat (The original "Rocky" movie, not the 18 sequels that followed)?

I was the poster boy for that old sports cliché, "It's not whether you win or lose, but how you played the game." Was this another one of those life lessons to be learned? Perhaps. Maybe so. Hell, I didn't know. I was 18 years old for crying out loud. My life was still in the first quarter of this worn-out sports cliché. Sometimes, because I was an 18-year-old teen-ager, I thought I had all the answers. Other times, whether I cared to admit it or not, I had noth'n. No clue. Let's just say in my most positive spin, win or lose, I was learning to keep my eyes and heart open to life's possibilities.

I can tell you this: That tremendous feeling of joy and freedom I was talking about experiencing on the football field?

It was so great it carried me right out the door at the end of the retreat and onto the highway as I drove back to school. It carried me right up to the moment I heard the siren and saw the cherry-top lights of a highway patrol car in my rear-view mirror. Incredibly, the patrolman who pulled me over was totally unsympathetic to my explanation of how the euphoria of the last couple of days had innocently contributed to my lead foot. I was cited for excessive speeding and hazardous driving (The grey skies had begun to unburden themselves of their snow).

Because this was not the first time I had seen flashing lights in my rear-view mirror, it was my ticket to driver's school and a day out of my life watching gruesome car crash films with my fellow dregs of society. You know, amongst all my "finding yourself" psychological and spiritual ruminations, perhaps a dose of common sense along the way would have been helpful as well. Who the hell ends up in driving school after attending a spiritual retreat? Some of us have a propensity to learn our lessons the hard way. I was 18 after all. Sigh.

And with that, I have to admit I'm about talked out. There's not much more I can say about this particular time in my life. Although, upon reading this, I'm sure I'll be reminded by my Oak Street family of a "how could you forget that?" incident. How exceptional or inspirational or enlightening this story is, I don't know. I'll leave that up to you. I'm satisfied I did the story justice without regrets. I was true.

Over the years that followed, my understanding and appreciation for dad's gift of infinite possibilities continued to grow. Along the way, you could say I carried with me a sense of responsibility to be a worthy recipient of his gift, to create a body of work befitting its fullest potential. To squander such a gift by ignoring it would be as much a tragedy as the loss of my father. There was no grand plan however. Sometimes I've overreached or misinterpreted, but his gift has infused my life with the glory of hope, and sustained me through victories and defeats. It's a privilege that inspires me to fight the good fight, to finish the race, to keep the faith. It's a gift I'm not sure I can ever live up to. I'll keep trying though. I'll keep praying to the Holy Spirit to light my life-path, my freedom road. I'll keep praying for the Spirit to fill me with the wisdom to discern the way and the strength to walk the revealed path leading to God's glory and Dad's honor.

Amen. Alleluia.

Postscript

"Like the pine trees linin' the windin' road...
I've got a name, I've got a name.

I carry it with me like my daddy did
But I'm livin' the dream that he kept hid.

Movin' mc down the highway...
Movin' ahead so life won't pass me by."

From the song "I've Got A Name"
By Jim Croce

A Poetic Journey To Cleveland and
Revisiting The Cemetery

In the summer of 2004, my wife, our youngest child and I flew to Cleveland, Ohio to attend a family reunion for my father's side of the family. We also used this trip as an opportunity to prevail upon my Uncle Jerry to act as tour guide and show us around the old neighborhood where he and dad grew up.

Now, I'm sensitive to the possibility that while you may have enjoyed my company thus far, a long recap of our visit to Cleveland might feel like overstaying my welcome. So I've attempted to give you our tour's highlights via the following poetic sound bite. Here is what I discovered:

A Cleveland Homecoming

I came to Cleveland in search of the west side story
of a depression-era baby,
a steel buyer's oldest son.

I search for my heritage
along the Brookside Park streets of the west side;
there you can find the monuments to my father's youth.
Blessed Sacrament of the old neighborhood
and Klein's Pharmacy on Fulton Street.
The faded history bricked and mortared
at the corner butcher shop,
a man for others forged on Carroll Street.

Riverside calls a fatherless son home.
3419 stands two-stories tall,
gable erect and front porch proud.
A young man gazes from the bay window.
I see his future
and know his life's journey.
Our futures and pasts become one,
healing my cinco de mayo broken heart.

I learn this west side story
is a story of hope.
Where the River of my bloodline first flowed
and the light of my soul first shown.
This is where the promise of my life
becomes the promise of my sons and daughters.
Riverside sends a father's son home.

Family reunions can be a little tricky. There's a reason they are generally held every couple of years or decade, whatever the case might be. Sometimes it takes that long to forget what you were reminded of about certain family members or had witnessed at the picnic. We Kansas Citians had a great time reminiscing and catching up with our extended Bickimer family. We spent just the right amount of time there to carry home with us fond memories and leave them calling for more. Yet the reunion I will cherish most occurred at 3419 Riverside. That's a reunion I won't soon forget.

It's the spring of 2010 and I'm stubbornly wandering around the cemetery like Moses in the desert. It's been a long time between visits. As I near the end of writing this book, I've come to realize I can't say I'm done telling the story until I make this trip. I'm a little chagrined I can't find it, and GPS is not going to help me here. I give up and stop by the funeral home to ask for directions.

Map in hand, I take the cemetery road to space 12, lot 323, block 18. All of the blocks have been given a name suitable for a person to contemplate one's place in eternity. My dad's gravesite happens to be located in "Garden of Open Bible." You should see some of the names for the cemetery blocks that are on the map. I'm tempted to do a whole riff speculating as to why you would be buried in, say, "The Garden of Peace" versus "Companion Garden." Were you a "people" person, or did you just want to be left alone? But I'll save the gallows humor for another time. It's a short walk up the grassy, shaded incline past grave markers of all shapes and sizes announcing many a life that passed here on earth. And then, yes, there it is. The red granite tombstone reads:

*"I shall walk forward into
the new day with God."*

Thomas E. Bickimer

February 5, 1932
May 5, 1974

Thomas Elwood Bickimer. Why on earth would grandma give her son a middle name like that? (As it turns out, my sister Leslie informs me "Elwood" was the name of the doctor who delivered dad. Well, I guess it could have been worse.) Actually I think it's a pretty cool name, made even more hip by Dan Aykroyd's character, Elwood Blues, in the movie "The Blues Brothers."

I notice a tombstone to the left of dad with no name or inscription. I'm thinking this must be mom's way of staking her claim for her rightful place beside dad and not a marker for the anonymous "player to be named later" that we never hear about in baseball trades. I can say with a pretty high degree of certainty that mom is not any great hurry to join him, but by God, she's prepared for that glorious day when she can be reunited with her Elwood.

While there, I hear the sound of the ground keepers' mowers and birds singing, the steady drone of locusts and the breeze rustling leaves in the nearby trees. That is all I hear. I see before me this grave marker with its inscribed name, and I see the surrounding pallet of colors and textures we know as Nature. And that is all I see. I turn to go, even start driving back up the road towards the entrance gates of the cemetery before I suddenly realize what I have missed.

Where were the pangs of regret, the pleading or the emotional rending that accompanied my previous visits to this place that holds such ambivalence for me? I turn around and go back. With my fingers I trace his name and inscription on the tombstone. "I shall walk forward into the new day with God." This was the last line from an inspirational saying that dad had liked and cut out of the newspaper one day long ago. From that day on, he carried it in his wallet as I too carry it in my wallet today. Under the protection of the grand old oak tree faithfully standing guard nearby, I take a moment to wonder if this is what it means to be at peace.

Epilogue

"I see Mary in the garden
In the garden of a thousand sighs
There's holy pictures of our children…

A dream of life comes to me…

Sky of love, sky of tears (a dream of life)
Sky of glory and sadness (a dream of life)
Sky of mercy, sky of fear (a dream of life)
Sky of memory and shadow (a dream of life)…

Sky of longing and emptiness (a dream of life)
Sky of fullness, sky of blessed life (a dream of life)

Come on up for the rising
Come on up, lay your hands in mine
Come on up for the rising
Come on up for the rising tonight"

From the song "The Rising"
By Bruce Springsteen

"As for me, the time has come to be gone.

I have fought the good fight to the end,

I have run the race to the finish;

I have kept the faith."

2 Timothy
4:6

Wayfarer

Hey, thanks for sticking with me all the way to the end of this saga. We covered a lot of ground together, and now here we are, back in the comfort of my study. I look up from where I'm seated at my desk, and with a rueful smile I notice a couple of dad's old pipes sitting on my bookshelf. Dad smoked a pipe around the house, a concession to Mom for not smoking cigarettes. Of course that night when he was admitted to the hospital, he confessed to smoking the damn things at work. The house is quiet, save the same ol' mantel clock's relentless, rhythmic counting of time. Spring has arrived, and a glorious sun-drenched day streams through my windows.

Music and the poetry of the written word are the Kodachrome for the expression of those feelings most important to my heart. I recently came across a wonderful poem by the Irish poet James Stephens. In the poem "Strict Care, Strict Joy" there is the line, "the poet makes grief beautiful." While I can't play an instrument or sing a lick, and don't claim to be much of a poet, I've always found my voice in the written word. Whether they were my own words or the words or lyrics of another, they resonate with me in some special way.

Putting words to paper was the best way I knew to tell my story. It was the reason why I included in this story pieces of songs and poems like Stephens' that have touched me over the years.

So with that same spirit in mind, here's a little something that just may help illustrate how nice it is outside today, and how good I feel inside:

Garden of Eden

I saw Him today.

Resplendent blossoms,
nature's symphony,
colored and hued.

Morning meadow grass,
dappled vivid green,
verdant and dewed.

Soaring boundless sky,
robin's eggshell blue,
bathed in ephemeral light.

I heard His life hymn today.
Hope, nature's eternal song.

I'm a little worried I committed some sort of literary faux pas by including a postscript and an epilogue in this book. Oh well, I'm not claiming to be the second coming of _____ (fill in your favorite author here). In fact, I debated whether or not to write this epilogue in the first place. You see on the one hand, I kept thinking that if I were you and had gotten this far, you would probably want to know what the hell happens to me between the then and now. Think of it as Paul Harvey's, "The rest of the story," if you will.

But on the other hand, here's the danger in wrapping things up in a nice and neat way: There's a temptation to get way to philosophical about things - I think you're at the breaking point anyway - and sour your experience of what may have been a good read up until now. The last thing I want to do is provoke a regret you picked this book up in the first place. Then to, there is the urge to write a Hollywood ending where I can point to one significant moment when I finally conquered my grief and lived happily ever after. Oh, if it were that easy. Nevertheless, let's throw caution to the wind and try to wrap things up in a way that gives you some measure of satisfaction, and me some comfort in knowing I stayed the course in telling my story.

So, upon graduating from high school, I found my true calling and became a WWF wrestling star. Just kidding. Joking aside, let me start by saying if you were to chart the progress of my coping skills from that black day in May of 1974, until the end of my story and beyond, it would NOT look like a steadily rising, never faltering, 45-degree angular line. No, what you'd see is something that looks closer to a Dow Jones Industrial Average Performance chart, up and down, up and down. Yet most importantly, you would see progress has been made. I couldn't have written this personal narrative otherwise.

Reading my story, you saw how I, to my detriment I might add, wasn't one to seek help or solace. Fortunately for me, despite my best intentions, there were those along the way who sought me out and provided friendship and support. They did it with such stealth and cunning that I often failed to recognize what they were doing for me until much later when it was too late to express my gratitude. But not too late to have convinced me I needed to work on not being so damn stubborn by bottling everything up inside when dealing with the more difficult times in my life. I acknowledge this continues to be a work in progress, but I have seen how shared grief is a good thing. It returns you quicker to those people and activities that give true happiness and peace of mind in your life.

Sometimes from out of the blue, I'm visited by a memory from those Oak Street days that will still cause my heart to ache, like the ache of that surgically-repaired knee announcing the threat of rain. But I can tell you my heart was mended by the love of that special girl mentioned in the retreat letter to myself. She remains, and will always be, the love of my life, and really, the only one who could ever put up with me. Yes, I got the girl, and I've been blessed with the titles of husband and father as well. I'm a better man for carrying those titles, and I continue to learn from the examples set by my wife and children.

I graduated from the University of Kansas in three years, married at the age of 21, and became a father at 22. Wow, was I young! I started what I modestly believe has been a successful business at the ripe old age of 24. In succeeding years, my family and responsibilities continued to grow at a dizzying rate. My circle of life rapidly expanded through an accumulation of trial, error and an abundance of blessings. I'm not telling you these things to brag, but to admit I rushed through the first 42 years of my life hell-bent on completing a never-ending to do list of my own making before the witching hour came. When it would all just be gone like the promise of a May day so long ago. It was presumptuous of me to think the age of 42 could hold the same significance for me as did for my dad. I've since learned to slow down a bit, to try to take the time to smell the roses along the way. Through the frenetic and serene of all my years since that May day, I've carried the hope that my father walked with me every step of the way. That he came to know his daughter-in-law and grandchildren. How I wish they could have had the chance to know my dad.

It is my hope that through this story you got to know a little bit about my father. All that remains of my father are photographs and the memories carried by those who knew him. As the years go by, fewer and fewer people carry those treasures. For many years, I played in a charity golf tournament named in honor of my father and sponsored by his old company. There was a satisfying bond I was grateful to share with those I saw during the event who knew dad and my family. I was proud to hear how much dad was admired and respected, and missed too.

But there came a year when I found myself surrounded by strangers. They were nice people, but they only knew dad's name, not the man. There's a familiar feeling of abandonment when something like that happens, a reminder of how I felt 36 years ago. So you move on, the years fly by, and then one day you receive a wonderful surprise. I happened to be serving on the Board of an area retirement community. At one of their functions, a resident approached me and introduced himself as someone who had done business with and known my father. Now that was a great feeling. These connections with the past, with dad, are so rare now. They are to be savored like a fine wine.

As of this writing, my mom is still alive, loved and appreciated by those who know her. She is the matriarch of a family that has grown to include a gang of grandchildren. They are the living legacy of the great love she shared with Elwood. And my brother and sisters? There are a lifetime of wistful regrets and hurt feelings, but there has also been forgiveness, tolerance, and even laughter along the way. Through it all there has been a current of empathy for each other born out of the familial bonds shared by siblings and fired by that singular life event we shared. Their stories are no less poignant than mine and someday deserve to be heard.

Then the day arrived when this story came bubbling up to the surface. It's a story that's never been told in its entirety, only told in bits and pieces stingily parceled out through the years. Until now, it's been a grief mostly unshared. It's a grief tucked away and hidden, a place not to be visited for fear of the consequences. Lord knows I didn't write this for your sympathy, and I didn't feel an overwhelming need at this point in my life to unburden my soul. It is what it is. It's been a labor of love, a calling I've tried to answer.

While writing this story, the thought crossed my mind that there could be this kind of residual fall-out where people who read this might see there is more to me than meets the eye. And that's ok, I think. I really tried to avoid being that word "pretentious" I mentioned way back in the Prologue. At the end of the day, I wrote this story because these words will live on long past the last person on earth who knew my Oak Street family has gone. Like James Stephens, I wanted to tell a story with "strict care" so I could make the grief in that seminal moment in time beautiful. At the end of the day, I wanted you to know I too bear witness to a faith proclaiming, "there is a time and a reason for every purpose under heaven." That picture of dad and me on my 16th birthday? Look closer. There behind dad, looking over his right shoulder, see the Sacred Heart of Jesus statue we as kids so often knelt before. I wanted you to see we were brave.

Oak Street Sojourn

Marbled entry to forty years of living,
Oak Street stands proud, quiet, empty.
Waiting for voices to make this a house a home,
it was for us a family sewn.

Bridge over troubled waters born free;
TE with pipe, heartfelt over the ivory.
Holiday feasts and obligatory pictures,
Dolphins ruin a Christmas dinner.

Our Father's prayer on unsteady knees,
car-ride light shows magic under the Christmas tree.
History watched in black, white and color,
the greater world's good and evil we discover.

Home-cooked meals lovingly prepared,
furtive phone talk on basement stairs.
Mom and Dad's bedroom becomes Mom's end of the hall,
where the grandchildren window watch for Santa Claus.

My room Mary-painted darkest blue,
here music and books colored my solitude.
Window scenes of cold gray Sunday skies
plumb the secret depths of who am I.

Said goodbye to this home and youth,
to find my way and seek the Truth.
A road less traveled, truth-seeds sewn,
richly yields a family, a home of my own.

I returned for the long goodbye,
to empty Oak Street's fading light.
Memories recalled and safely stored,
only silence remains as I close the door.

By TJB

About The Author

Husband, father, son, brother, uncle, Catholic, contractor, philanthropist, writer, golfer, friend. Further description would require writing a book, and I just don't have it in me right now.

Currently, Tom does not live on a street named after a tree. If you would like to contact him, you may do so by writing to him at P.O. Box 7431, O.P., Ks. 66207 or visiting the website promiseoflearning.com. Oak Street will always live on in his heart.

The Promise of Learning Foundation

P.O. Box 7431

Overland Park, Ks.   66207

The Promise of Learning Foundation was formed as a 501C3 not-for-profit organization in 1997. The primary mission of the Foundation is to provide time, talent and financial assistance to those individuals, institutions and programs who share our belief that education offers our greatest hope and best means for underprivileged children and young adults to realize their potential and dreams. In recent years, our mission has expanded to include support for emergency relief services in third world countries experiencing profound loss and hardship from natural disasters or civil unrest.

For further information, visit our website at;
promiseoflearning.com.

Please consider making a donation to this worthy organization. 100% of your donation goes directly to those who we support. Thank you.

www.ingramcontent.com/pod-product-compliance
Lightning Source LLC
Chambersburg PA
CBHW020508040426
42331CB00042BA/95